A Multicultural BRIDGE Living History Project

All rights reserved

Published by Multicultural BRIDGE

No part of this publication may be reproduced
in whole or in part, or stored in a retrieval system, or
transmitted in any form or by any means, electronic,
mechanical, photocopying, recording, or otherwise,
without written permission from publisher.

This book is to be used strictly for fundraising or
eductional purposes. All proceeds to benefit
Multicultural BRIDGE a 501c3 organization

For information regarding permission, write to:

Multicultural BRIDGE
Permissions
17 Main Street, Suite 2
Lee, MA 01238

Text copyright PENDING by Multicultural BRIDGE
Cover & Content Design by Nik Davies
Cover photo by JV Hampton VanSant
Naumkeag, Stockbridge, MA
Trustees of the Reservations

ISBN: 978-0-9908282-0-4
Library of Congress Control Number:

Contents

i	Preface
vi	Collaboration
23	Celebration
41	Learning
71	Integration
99	Empowerment
131	Appendix
135	Photo Gallery

In Loving Memory
of
Josephine & Wilbur Johnson
Sallie VanSant

♥

For Sam, JV, Jessica, Maya and Westley, Annie, Barbara and Will. With deepest appreciation, love and gratitude for each of you and the inspiration you give me each day.

♥

Thank you to all of the angels that have crossed my life's path and contributed to the creation of *Berkshire Mosaic* and my story.

About Berkshire Mosaic

♥

In January 2012, Multicultural BRIDGE and its Race Task Force hosted a film screening and facilitated discussion of RACE–The Power of an Illusion by California Newsreel. It was a three-part series previously aired on PBS that we showcased at the Triplex Cinema, Beacon Cinema, and Images Cinema. After viewing an excerpt at an "Undoing Racism" training in Boston, I strategically made the film accessible to all residents of Berkshire County to begin to unpack the social construct of race, its history and the current social conditions influenced by this systematic approach to create and preserve wealth and privilege.

It was when Kate Abbott attended one of these series that I discovered our shared aspiration of honoring the diverse heritage of the Berkshires and our mutual love of connecting with people. So, as stewards of our collective humanity, we cooked up an On the BRIDGE collaboration between the Berkshire Eagle and Multicultural BRIDGE. Throughout this process, many times I have been reminded of Reverend Dr. Martin Luther King Jr.'s sage advice, "Human progress is neither automatic nor inevitable. Every step toward the goal of justice requires sacrifice, suffering and struggle; the tireless exertions and passionate concern of dedicated individuals."

With a goal of portraying a gentle, inviting, celebratory yet powerful form of social justice, I carefully hand-selected these unique stories that have appeared in the Berkshire Eagle's Berkshire Week and Shires of Vermont magazine. These stories have been penned for us by our team, Kate Abbott, Elizabeth Blackshine, Siobhan Connally, Nik Davies, Kuukua Dzigbordi Yomekpe, JV Hampton-VanSant, Roberta McCulloch Dews, Emma Sanger Johnson, Jenn Smith and Margot Welch. They have afforded time and space to each individual to tell their own story, to shine their own light.

For the team, nothing has been more richly authentic and engaging than listening to and deeply hearing another's journey, hopes, and dreams. This team, each fired by our desire to understand, hear and see people in our community is driven by our compassion and desire to have others see, hear and understand these stories. We have learned what it really means to "meet on the bridge" and to journey, to heal and to grow together through storytelling. Each contributing writer's written pieces flow together to create our unique collective narrative—the story of our Berkshire Mosaic.

We each have been honored by the privilege of sharing in another's living history, capturing a snapshot into a specific moment in life.

After publishing these stories, one by one, in our local paper, I realized more people needed to read these stories and have the opportunity to see our community through this mosaic lens. Nik Davies, Multicultural BRIDGE Executive Vice President of Governance and local Berkshire author and columnist, stepped forward to join me with enthusiasm as Editor-in-Chief and so the Berkshire Mosaic: A Multicultural BRIDGE Living History Project was launched. I welcome you on our journey!

Gwendolyn Hampton VanSant

CEO, Founding Executive Director
Multicultural BRIDGE

Living History Project

♥

    This book is a wonderful addition to any bookshelf. It presents a picture of the Berkshires that highlights the region's multicultural heritage. The stories contained in this book reveal the ways in which the history and present-day climate in the Berkshires have been shaped by the contributions of a diverse group of individuals. Profiles of men and women, young and old, illustrate the power of the individual to make a difference in their local communities by bringing new perspectives, wellsprings of energy and fresh ideas, and a determination to effect positive changes for everyone.

    Readers will learn about projects designed to empower and mentor local youth, as well as the work of artists, scholars, and business owners who are all committed to enhancing daily life in the Berkshires. At the same time, the stories presented on these pages remind us that issues of diversity and tolerance have long been important to so many residents of the Berkshires since the eighteenth and nineteenth centuries. Indeed, readers might consider the ways in which the people profiled in this book are connected to the legacies of both Elizabeth Freeman, the enslaved woman from Sheffield, Massachusetts who successfully sued for her freedom in 1780 and Great Barrington's native son, W. E. B. DuBois.

    This book is a treasure because it offers readers the opportunity to learn about the region's racial, ethnic, linguistic, religious, cultural, and international diversity. The profiles on these pages allow readers to connect with a wide range of individuals and also give us the chance to think about the ways in which our experiences and goals so often overlap with theirs. By calling attention to the rich and vibrant multicultural heritage of the Berkshires, this book reminds us of each person's potential to enhance and contribute to our local communities.

Barbara Krauthamer

Professor African American History
University of Massachusetts at Amherst
The NAACP Image Award for
Outstanding Literary Work

Note from the Editor-in-Chief

♥

As a fiction writer, I've spent most of my life creating worlds. Worlds I've imagined and buried within typewritten pages and covered in fancy artwork. For me, it was far easier to create imaginary places than to face the inequities of a real world I felt too small and insignificant to change.

Although I hoped and believed that someone would come along to bridge the gaps that so many people fall through, I wasn't quite willing to build those bridges myself. Then one day, by chance or providence, I met Gwendolyn Hampton VanSant, a woman who was building bridges, piece by piece with her own hands. She showed me that, within me, I too can fill the gaps; to spread right, leverage change and positively impact the structure of the world around me.

Working with Gwendolyn and the inspiring people that comprise Multicultural BRIDGE, I have discovered that I can make a difference in our world by simply being me, no matter how small and insignificant I think I am. I can bring about change by learning, celebrating, integrating, collaborating and empowering every individual I see and touch. I can do it, and so can you.

My soul is strengthened knowing that via this *Berkshire Mosaic*; I am helping shed light on a small portion of the many beautiful faces that make up our diverse world. I sincerely hope that you enjoy getting to know the incredible people within these pages and I pray that this anthology will inspire you to venture out into this world and help build the bridges that will link people together. Go out and spread love, light and inclusion, and appreciate every individual for their personal uniqueness. Let us all celebrate life, love and the intricate mosaic we craft when we all stand together as one.

Enjoy!

Nik Davies

Young Adult Fiction Author
Multicultural BRIDGE EVP of Governance

Introduction

♥

"The most important thing to remember is this: To be ready at any moment to give up what you are for what you might become." - W.E.B. Du Bois

It is with such great pleasure that I know that this book has fallen into your hands and that you will be so deeply touched by the individuals and their families that you are about to meet. These stories create the mosaic of the Berkshire Hills and also reflect the mosaic of our country. Find yourself within these pages.

Why the metaphor of the Mosaic? It is because, in all of our fragmented pieces of various objects and materials, some fuller than others, some shiny, some dulled over time, we make up a beautiful piece of artwork. We each are a part of a larger whole. This is what we must remember. In an assimilationist mindset, recent generations consider the United States a melting pot. However, as was explained in the *Race: the Power of an Illusion* documentary, some of us in our American history were only afforded the role as "embers for the melting pot". In this anthology, a multiculturalist mindset that allows for each culture to share its values, maintain its language and traditions as we all learn from one another. This marks a shift in the values for our country founded on religious freedom and heralded for upholding constitutional rights. We are all immigrants here on this land—by choice or not, by migration or slavery.

Over the last several years, I have been charged with this ministry of connecting people, their stories, within community. When I fully open my eyes, heart, and ears, I changed my path in life and took on this servant leadership role that I would have never imagined if not guided by my own deep listening. My passion is deconstructing systemic racism, classism, and sexism; revealing the impact of these systems within our communities. I hope to lead us into awareness and consciousness so we each catalyze new systems that level the playing field promoting social justice, equity and the humanity of each individual. I have wholeheartedly claimed this as my ministry, this ministry of knowing people, seeing each person's humanity and their strengths, hearing truths untold and having the capacity of knowing with full compassion. And then sharing that all broadly in our Berkshire community.

One participant after a training session captured why I truly do this work when she thanked me for allowing her the space to get in touch with her own humanity. We sometimes get lost in the buzz of the day--work, chores, responsibilities, internet, technology, finances, media, etc. And really what we crave is making human connections.

We have to be willing to have tough conversations, stand up for what we believe in, and to leave a community stronger than the one we found. I have experienced the pains associated with systemic racism and the intersections of class, gender and race, and the places where our mutual humanity has been forgotten. I know what it is like to be deemed invisible and to feel unheard as a mother and a woman. That knowing is what fuels my work, my ministry. Equally, I also know what it is to be held in community by loved ones and by neighbors and strangers. I know what it is to be valued for my strengths and experience and that is the gift this anthology bears. This Mosaic brings out the beauty of all of our stories that make up the whole of the Berkshires.

I think of a dear friend and colleague that said, "I grew up in Berkshire County all of my life and it wasn't until I met Gwendolyn that I figured out I mattered, that I had a place here and had something to offer." A mature African American woman with a family legacy of over one hundred years of Berkshire history said those words to me.

The Berkshires is a place of incredible beauty and opportunity for connection and healing. In the words of Margaret

J. Wheatley, "Such healing is possible because, in all our diversity, we share the experience of being human. We each have the same longings and feelings. We each feel fear, loneliness, and grief. We each want to be happy and to live a meaningful life. We discover this shared human experience whenever we listen to someone's unique story…as we listen quietly to their story, as we allow another's life to be different from ours, suddenly we find ourselves on common ground. *(Turning to One Another*, p. 118)

I have high hopes for this *Berkshire Mosaic* anthology to create connectedness for those near and far. We can be proud of how the Berkshires can and does embrace our diverse heritage. How we can and do welcome new residents. This Mosaic reflects the dreams, struggles, sacrifices and accomplishments attached to each of these stories. This is our living history here in the Berkshires and also in the United States. My dream is for our Berkshire community to be a model for other communities honoring that we each have a story to be told and we each have a place to claim.

If you are a student or an educator, be inspired. If you are a youth or young at heart, be empowered. If you are a parent, grandparent, cousin, aunt or uncle, be nostalgic and proud. I invite you to experience the immense power of storytelling as you read the *Berkshire Mosaic: A Living History Project*. The stories speak for themselves, they need no further introduction.

Gwendolyn

Gwendolyn & Sam VanSant

Collaboration

Building bridges between our divisions

I reach out to you,

Will you reach out to me?

With all our voices,

With all our visions,

Friends, we could make such sweet harmony.

~ Contemporary English Quaker Round

Collaborative Heart Mosaic
Created by Stearns Elementary Students
BRIDGE Artist in Residence ~ Karen Woolis

Satyana Ananda

by Siobhan Connally

Satyana Ananda knows that sometimes the worst thing that can happen to a person isn't the worst thing at all. Sometimes the worst thing can be a miracle. That's part and parcel of Satyana's mission as director of the Starseed Sanctuary, an interfaith healing and retreat center she has operated from her home in the Berkshires since the late 1980s.

All along it's been a struggle. A struggle to find a place, to stay on the land and to create a haven for healing energy. Originally from Ohio, she was raised Catholic and practiced devoutly until the age of 26 when she found Hinduism. She had been living in Boston with her husband and three children when they founded Survival Co-Op and World Union Center, where she sought to introduce people to the benefits of yoga, meditation, and natural foods. It was the early seventies. "There was a moment when we all gathered in one room to make a prayer before we ate and in that moment that energy channeled through me I began to speak the blessing. People from all walks, all spiritual paths, were there. There was an incredible spirit of oneness."

Though the Boston center didn't survive, lasting only about a year, the seed for her life's work was sewn.

"It took another decade before we found this place," she said, noting that during that time she trained in all aspects of nature's healing arts, as well as explored her development as a lay minister within the Unitarian Church. When she found the 130-acre property in Savoy, she knew she'd found her center. And over the years her center has grown from within, with a spacious carriage house that is used as a spiritual center; with a main dwelling featuring a large, open-style farm kitchen and dormitory-style accommodations for groups and individuals. She runs all kinds of programs for people in transition. People who are searching for answers from within.

"What I do here at Starseed involves leading ceremonies on Equinox, Solstices and other key energetic times. I lead other ceremonies as well; weddings, rites of passage, retreats. We are doing more and more personal guided retreats where people come for a day or a week, or sometimes longer. We find out what they need and then we provide it. It's a holistic retreat. We line them up with food, movement, emotional, body, energy balancing, earth-based healing, spiritual direction and life coaching." She's also facilitated a popular program for women ages 50 and beyond called "Coming to the Well."

"My life purpose is founded in my coming from the four root races: African, Native American, European and Asian. Part of my purpose is to create an environment, a sanctuary and experiences where people can feel that we are all one. That we all came from the same place and that we are all connected. Starseed is that sacred container where healing can take place."

"It's not just one aspect of healing. Not just physical, not just emotional, spiritual but also mental so all of the bodies get addressed." Groups of like minds have also rented Starseed's homey retreat house for their own wellness and spiritual programs. But occasionally there have been problems.

"We once had a group of men here from New York City who were doing a kind of vision quest. I didn't feel as if they were taking care of the land and I asked them about it. The men, they had a fire one night and the next day after they had left, my husband and I saw smoke. The whole field had burned up to the woods."

She was devastated and couldn't look away from the fire's damage. So she began to sweep away the ashes. Her husband joined her, and soon they found a rose quartz stone among the ashes, which had been engraved with the word *miracle*.

Satyana at Starseed Sanctuary

"And that's what I decided it was, a miracle. Especially after we swept away the ashes and found these beautiful stones just over there. We call them our Grandfather Stones. When you sit with them, you sit with your ancestors."

Today, Satyana's daughters are helping her achieve the next phase for Starseed. They are helping to transition Starseed from a retreat center into a place that will include more of an intentional community. She envisions land stewards who will take a few acres of land to start an agricultural program—perhaps a CSA that will grow food and medicinal herbs. Her plan includes Interfaith meetings in counsel format where contributing members make decisions about all aspects of the center from planned housing to sanctuary maintenance, trail building, and agriculture. But ultimately, her goal is to spread light and harmony to the community. "I see a lot of people who come here who are at a crossroads. They are in crisis and they need to make an inner shift. And what they need is to connect with the spiritual part of themselves. In nature, they can feel their oneness, the beauty and the perfection of nature. By being in that energy field, it opens them to the work we do together. It expands their experience of the world."

> "Part of my purpose is to create an environment, a sanctuary and experience where people can feel that we are all one."

Professor Sandra Burton & Dr. Don Quinn Kelley

by Liz Blackshine

Big love—the bonds that shape a life, links that intertwine and hold a community. Love that is old, tried, and exuberant. These are the phrases that come to mind after peeling back the surface of the lives of two people who've been an integral part of the Berkshires community since the 1980s. Two of the original steering committee members and co-chairs of Lift Ev'ry Voice, the Berkshires' fine-arts summer-long celebration of African-American culture, are a married couple: Sandra Burton, a professor at Williams College and chair of the Dance Department, and Dr. Don Quinn Kelley, historian and Professor Emeritus at Medgar Evers College at the City University of New York. They grew up in the throes of the civil rights era, and they draw deeply from the legacy of love vested to them by their elders.

"Peace, love, respect for everybody. The only time you look down on someone is when you help them up," they said in unison, reciting the motto taught to them by the Chuck Davis Dance Company, an African American dance ensemble Professor Burton has danced with for many years. Originally from the South Bronx, she came to the Berkshires in the 1970s to perform at Jacob's Pillow, and she got a residency at Williams College. Eventually, she accepted a faculty position at the college and then officially moved to the area in 1984.

"I was raised to try to learn where you are," said Professor Burton, "try to meet people, try to connect with them, and see what's going on. I saw that the county is spread out...getting to know people was hard. You really had to work at it. And I did. We'd go to the schools and we'd introduce ourselves to the principals and to the teachers and say, 'what are you doing, do you need any programming?' That way we got to know parents, students, the secretaries, the cafeteria workers, and that really grew my affection for what's really here, and I started to do programming at Williams College that spoke to that."

She has a contagious passion for supporting people and building community stemming from her involvement with Camp Minisink, started by a small group of African-American teachers and public service workers. Camp Minisink is an after-school program located in Harlem with 600 acres in upstate New York for camping and other programming.

"We were expected to be engaged in community life no matter where you are," she said. "You look around and you see where you can contribute, to help somebody else because you're being helped. And it left a deep life impression on me."

With tearing eyes and in deep appreciation and reflection on the camp directors and counselors, she said, "We got comfortable with other people in the world. The directors at the camp wanted the children to have that type of familiarity, not to be raised in fear of other people who didn't look like you. Three years ago we had a reunion in New York, and people came from all over the world and, you know, we looked at each other and we burst into tears...because it's rich. It gave us strength. It gave us strength to take the blow and keep going that people will spit on you and hit you, but inside they can't touch you. They taught us to never be ashamed of being black."

Similarly, Dr. Kelley, originally from Chicago, was raised with elders who instilled a deep sense of pride, self-love, and independent thinking. His parents gave him each of his names after successfully influential black men that came before him. "Don" is from French Black writer Alexander Dumas' 1831 play, "Don Juan of Marana", "Quinn" comes from the Dr. William Paul Quinn, a Bishop of the African Methodist Episcopal Church in the 19th Century, who traveled the nation starting schools and churches.

Dr. Kelley's father often spoke to his children of the tragedies the family endured, stories passed down from his great-grandfather who was enslaved. Dr. Kelley remembers his father frequently reading the first edition of the English translation of the Koran, Karl Marx's Das Kapital, and the Bible. His mother was a Sunday school teacher.

"I always think of that song we sang there, 'Jesus Loves the Little Children, all the children of the world; red and yellow, black and white, they are precious in his sight...' that was human rights being taught to us, that all were equal before God, you know, and so my parents were very sophisticated." He later discovered in old letters from the 1950s addressed to his mother that she was a regular host for leaders of African countries struggling for their political freedom. In one of the most influential events in his life, his mother took him to view the body of a 14-year-old fellow Chicago youth, Emmett Till, who was brutally killed and mutilated for whistling at a white woman during his visit to Mississippi.

> *"Peace, love and respect for everybody. The only time you look down on anyone is when you help them up."*

"That affected me more than anything else in my youth," Dr. Kelley said. Emulating his parents' actions, while still in junior high school, curious to make sense of the contradictions in society he saw, and wanting to get active in finding answers to such atrocities, he sought out the Nation of Islam.

"I went to hear Elijah Mohammed, but [instead] I heard Malcolm X, and that year I started organizing young people. The notion was that you would go talk to people and after talking to them you'd have some type of understanding. The first [place] we went to was a program at a Catholic school. [Then] we went to a blind white woman's house. We had a great conversation. So we left, and the next day her house was bombed."

Inspired by the motto his father often told him, "He who thinks cannot be made a slave," Dr. Kelley took the legacy of activism and community contribution from his parents and, after undergraduate college, finished his doctorate in just three years. He is one of the founding faculty at the Medgar Evers College of the City University of New York.

"I used the 'Strength to Love' by Martin Luther King, Jr. as a base. It's a book of his sermons. And in that book he says it takes a strong person to love, that weak people give up or give in," he said. "So if you love someone, you have to be strong for them."

"With us, military service was just what everybody did," says Harold P. French, Jr., whose family has lived in Stockbridge for generations. "My grandfather was a Civil War vet and my daughter and my niece, working on lineage, have found Frenches serving all the way back to the Revolution."

Drafted right after high school graduation in 1965, French joined the Navy and served through the Vietnam War and beyond, until 1989 in the Construction Battalion. Seabees (CB's) have been building bases, bulldozing and paving miles of roads and airstrips, and executing military construction projects since World War II. "The Navy runs great schools. Every time they offered a course—Naval Aviation, Aircraft Engine Mechanics, Nuclear, Chemical and Biological Warfare, I signed up."

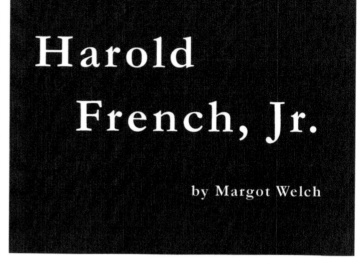

Harold French, Jr.

by Margot Welch

A lifelong learner and school volunteer, Harold always tells young people to focus on education. Recently commended for his volunteer commitments in Stockbridge, maybe he's been following his father's lead. "My Dad was the ultimate patriot. You didn't mess with his flag! Over the years, he worked as part-time police officer, school custodian, playground and lunchroom monitor, ambulance driver, and evenings and weekends caretaker. He always carried a first-aid kit. And we always had a garden, two cows, and chickens everywhere."

Regularly devoting time and energy to helping veterans, he is active with the American Legion, Semper Fi Families, Stand Down, and Soldier On. These programs, characterized by helpfulness, patriotism, and continuing devotion to fellow service members and veterans, aim to meet many urgent needs for food and clothing, housing, comprehensive

> *"Lots of guys have PTSD and they're not getting treated. When we signed up, they told us if we completed our obligations to the military, we'd have good health care for life. Today, vets are misunderstood, mistreated, and neglected."*

physical and mental health services, and employment. Harold focuses on re-entering veterans who are challenged by homelessness and PTSD.

"Lots of guys have PTSD and they're not getting treated. When we signed up, they told us if we completed our obligations to the military, we'd have good health care for life. Today, vets are misunderstood, mistreated, and neglected." Now, he explains, military pensions are no longer adequate to live on. Bases have been closed. That's hard for those families who moved to military communities for their services. Health insurance coverage is not universally accepted,

> "My grandfather was a Civil War vet and [we] have found Frenches serving all the way back to the Revolution."

and good treatment is hard to access.

"I've always been action-oriented. Even after I made rank, I'd never ask anyone to do something I wasn't going to do right along with them. And these guys are in the same boat I was in once. If they know you're a vet, they'll open up. People don't understand that the military is a real job. When you sign up for it, you're signing a blank check that everything you've got in your life belongs to your country."

Like joining the military, helping people was also what Frenches did. Since 1972, Harold has been a mainstay of the Stockbridge Grange—a source of fellowship, service projects and support to the community since the nineteenth century.

"The Grange movement started at the end of the Civil War," he explains, "to unite agriculturists around a common cause. A strong bond, like a union, helped farmers fight the railroads for fair grain storage and transport fees. They discovered that if they got together, traded ideas and plans, farmers could feed themselves."

"I'm glad we know how to grow our own food," he continues. "I'm a member of Future Farmers of America (FFA). When bad things happen, how will all the city people eat? Stockbridge used to have twenty-five dairy farms! Every Thursday we'd bring cases of milk to Lee so they could go for lab testing. Once I learned how to check sediment, smell, flavor, and butterfat, I could tell if milk had come from a clean barn, been left out in the sun, and cows fed on eating green grass and sweet silage. It was delicious!"

Deeply grateful to be alive especially after a genetic defect ruptured his aorta and a grandnephew miraculously saved his life, Harold thinks ahead joyfully to the family Thanksgiving celebration at the Grange and his children's futures. "I lived to hug my little great granddaughter and get to know my new great grandchildren!"

If much of the world has changed, much that is good and strong endures. How lucky for Stockbridge residents to have Harold P. French, Jr., the Can Do Seabee, as his cap proclaims, working hard alongside them until jobs get done.

♥

On the second floor of Pittsfield's First Baptist Church, Hilary Greene, Director of the Berkshire Immigrant Center (BIC), sits at her desk, stacked high with files, papers, and photos of her family and a horse she loved when she was growing up. She was nine when, with her family—both parents were teachers—moved from Brooklyn, New York to Hancock, Massachusetts. For them, Western Massachusetts was a new world, as it is for immigrants who come to BIC for help. We all know this story: people leave home for their children's futures to struggle, hope, work for better lives. Today they need citizenship preparation, tutoring, help completing visa applications, changes in status, and legal support. These tasks all take time, money, transportation and clarification - resources often inaccessible to immigrants working two jobs. Having fled wars, prisons, kidnappings, refugee camps, and violence, many need safety, work, housing, health care, legal assistance, literacy, and legitimacy.

Thirty years ago, Hilary's tenth-grade Monument Mountain Social Studies teacher paired her class with Russian penpals in Petrodvorets, a small town near St. Petersburg. She wrote to Olga and, months later with lines blacked out by a Cold War censor, her Russian friend's answer arrived. Both girls, wanting to master each other's language, exchanged long letters for six years. Just before Hilary's senior year at college, where she majored in Soviet and Russian Studies, she met Olga and her parents at St. Petersburg's Pulkovo airport, face to face. Tears of joy fell all around.

Having always loved history and languages, Hilary and a colleague set off to live in Olga's world two years after the Soviet Union dissolved. Foreign businesses were flooding into Russia: people were thrilled to meet Americans.

"It was 1991 and everyone wanted to practice speaking English! Every day was an adventure. I walked everywhere, rode buses and trains to last stops, explored neighborhoods, and had this deep sense of history, beauty, amazement: I was actually there!" Before arriving, Hilary and her friend had discovered Prague's new English Language newspaper and decided they would create one in St. Petersburg.

> "I have strong memories, deep feelings about the people that took care of me in a foreign country. [They] helped me, wanted to get to know me."

"It still exists! Even online now (sptimes.ru/) with our winged lion logo! After a year, we handed it off to other expats and started another business, Personnel Corps, placing English-speaking Russians in new jobs. Then I wrote for magazines and planned events for a big PR firm."

She smiles, remembering. "I was young like the new Russia! There was nothing I couldn't do!" However, for

Hilary Greene

by Margot Welch

most Russians, these times were miserable.

"Much was rationed. Everything was very expensive. Heating and plumbing systems broke down. I saw people standing in bread lines for hours, leaving with nothing but a broken egg. Highly educated professionals, doctors, teachers, lawyers, were earning less than the equivalent of $100 a month. Not enough to live on." How had the Russians survived a century's hardships, two World Wars and decades of the Cold War?

"Resilience, adaptability, and strength! They seem ingrained deep in Russian culture. I saw such generosity in Olga's family, and everywhere. If something broke, or someone needed something, there were networks, always someone to help exchange resources, make do, share whatever they had, trust their capacities to fix things without the government."

In 1996, Hilary came home, determined to find ways to keep using her Russian to make a positive difference in people's lives. After managing a Young Composers' Competition at Williams, she was hired by the Jewish Federation's New American and Refugee Resettlement Coalition that served Jewish refugees then leaving the Soviet Union. In 2002, when US policy shifted focus to Somalia, the Sudan, and other war-torn countries, that local program became the Berkshire Immigrant Center (berkshireic.com)

Marge Cohan & Hilary

"I have strong memories, deep feelings about the people who took care of me in a foreign country. [They] helped me, wanted to get to know me. It's important that I continue to do that for others here." Hilary and three colleagues work overtime at BIC where client numbers are higher than ever.

"We're at capacity in terms of the numbers of people we can serve," she says, adding that the search for funding never stops, and prospects for immigration reform now seem dim. "And what I hate most," she says, "is when people come with problems for which there is really no solution."

People desperate to bring in a spouse, sibling, child, parent, or grandparent face heartbreaking facts. Such petitions take twelve years. While Berkshire County's population and labor force are diminishing, dependence on immigrant workers grows. BIC's trainings have tempered anti-immigrant feelings. But in slow economies immigrants are vulnerable. But sometimes history, opportunity, and values coincide. Every day, new Americans are working hard, buying homes, paying taxes, starting businesses, strengthening our communities, and, like Hilary, feeling grateful.

"I love that every day is different. And, finishing a day's work, I love knowing that because our organization exists, someone else's life is a little easier. Watching devastated people get back on their feet, understanding courage—it's a privilege. I can't imagine doing anything else."

On a sunny afternoon, Brian Hicks goes fishing with his older son at Onota Lake. On a sunny and colder afternoon, he may drive to Ashley Falls or to Alford, on icy back roads, to help a housebound patient under doctor's orders to have blood drawn. Brian has two sons, 4 and 8 years old, who visit him in the summers. Last summer, he said, he took his older son to a Red Sox game to have his photo taken with Big Papi, and got his son baseball cards before the game, so his son would know all the players. He remembers that carefully planned day with a glow of laughter and energy.

Energy and planning have brought him a long way. This winter, Pittsfield awarded him Best of Pittsfield in the Medical Laboratory category. He has an extensive background in medical laboratory sciences, 10 years in the field and two master's degree in medical laboratory science and in business administration. And he has an unusual business model.

Brian D Hicks, MLS

by Kate Abbott

He saw a need, he saw doctors frustrated because lab tests results come back so slowly or because patients were slow to have the tests done, and he saw people who were in pain, or trapped by the snow, or unwilling to go to a doctor when they needed one. And he saw an innovative way to meet the need. Brian brings the tests to them.

In August 2012, he founded Clean Image, a 24-hour mobile medical lab. His is a unique kind of business, especially in the northern half of the country. He came to the Berkshires from Houston, Texas, and before that from Atlanta, Ga.

"I always had a passion for the medical field," He said. Born in Tennessee, he volunteered at a local hospital in high school and worked as a rehab aide while in college in Atlanta. He worked in hospital maintenance, and he was accepted into a one-year medical technology program at the University of Florida in Jacksonville, covering the usually two-year internship at high speed. Then he visited medical schools. He had always wanted to go to medical school. But as he considered the seven or more years of school still to come, he decided he would rather start to work immediately, and travel, and work with people, and start his own business.

He began a consulting business in Houston, which he still runs, often working with clients in New York. He earned an MBA and is working toward a doctorate in business with a specialty in health insurance.

Coming to North Adams on a chance

"Being a Medical Laboratory Scientist is more than just a career, it's a passion."

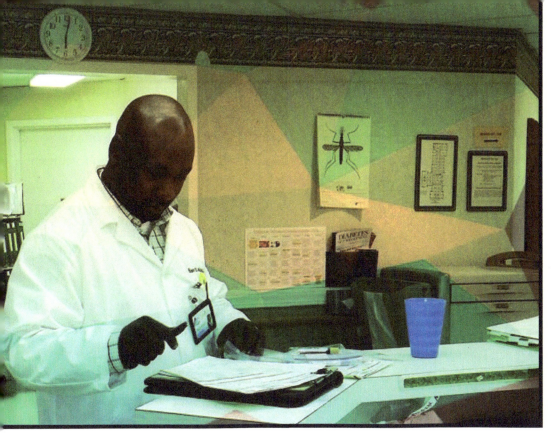

assignment, he decided the Berkshires could be fertile ground to build a new business. Clean Image has grown quickly, he said, with a combination of inside knowledge and technology.

"I can do everything from my phone," he said: schedule patients, take orders securely, deliver confidential results. Because he is a medical laboratory scientist, hospitals will work with him and insurance will cover his tests. The judicial system will refer people to him for drug screenings. Parents trying to get a child back will get screened to prove to family services that they are free of illegal drugs and alcohol. Through diligent networking, he said, he has expanded to cover a 50-mile radius outside the Berkshires, from Hartford, Connecticut, to Albany, New York

He can draw blood samples, run screens for drugs, tests for STDs, allergy or breast cancer panels, pre-screenings for men's health and more. He does not diagnose, he emphasized. If he sees anything out of the ordinary in a test result, he will promptly refer the patient to a doctor to look into it.

"I respect doctors," he said. Some people come to him for privacy, he said. Some come because it's cheaper, depending on their health insurance.

> "When it's your own business, you work harder. It's your baby, and you have more flexibility."

Some are house-bound by the ice, or from illness, and they welcome a lab that will come to them. If he draws blood on a doctor's order, he added, that service is free for the patient. People can come with a physician's order or pay out-of-pocket, Brian said. He offers discounts and payment plans and he has helped people who have no health insurance, or not enough, to find care. He often works with Porchlight VNA in Lee and with Jeffrey Kellogg, a physician's assistant with Berkshire Mobile Medicine, who does house calls. "When it's your own business, you work harder," he said. "It's your baby, and you have more flexibility." He has met obstacles, he said. Because his service is unique in New England, it is unfamiliar to many people. But he loves it, and he never gives up.

"It's a passion," he said. "It helps me to get up every day to have a go at it."

In 2009, Ann LaBier of Lee first went to Ireland on a 10-day trip in March, and she spent St. Patrick's Day in the town where her grandmother was born. Her grandparents—her father's parents and her mother's father, came to Brooklyn, New York, from Ireland in the early 1900s. Her grandmother came from Ballinrobe, County Mayo in Western Ireland.

The town is about as large as Lee, a downtown area surrounded by farmland and sheep. Ann saw the holiday parade there. St. Patrick's Day, she said, is a national holiday in Ireland and a religious holiday. Many people go to church in the morning after their chores are done.

Ann LaBier & Jo Grossman

by Kate Abbott

"There are parades everywhere," she said, and people dressed in costume, holding banners. The processions had themes like the recession, events shaping the town and communities. "It was breathtaking," she said, "to be standing on a street with 2,000 people and wondering how many were my relatives." At the South Mayo Family Research Center, she asked about her maiden name, Dulin, and that led Ann and her husband to the town of Doolin, on the Atlantic Coast near the Aran Islands. She remembers stone walls marking field borders, thatched roofs, piles of peat drying for fuel, and the bright colors of the houses, vibrant purples and yellows and green. Those colors, she was told, show independence.

"The government owns the houses," she said, "and once people pay them off, then they can paint them."

Ireland has gone through difficult times since her grandparents left although the country's entry into the European Union has helped recently. "Their stability is based on people coming," she said.

People like Jo Grossman of Housatonic, who has been visiting Ireland, for many years. She works for a foreign literary rights agency and travels often, and Ireland continually draws her back.

"It envelopes you," she said. "It makes you feel you belong there." She fell in love with the idea of Ireland when she was 12," she said. She has no Irish blood she knows of; her family is Jewish from Hungary and Germany, but she has loved the country for decades and visited many times. On her first trip, in 1993, many of the most famous sites were open, and she could walk right up to them.

She saw the green mounds at New Grange, she said, earth domes over passage graves. A small rock window sits above the low door, and at the summer solstice the sun shines through. Now tourism is growing, she said, and people are coming in. In Dublin, she learned to say "Thank you" in Polish from a young man who filled her car with petrol. But she likes the country and the smaller towns. "You battle sheep," she said. "They think they own the road." It mists often but rarely rains hard, she said, and "even when it rains, the colors look brighter." In June, the days stay light until

Warren LaBier, Rep. Smitty Pignatelli and Ann LaBier

11p.m. in the long, northern dusk. Music at the pubs starts late, she said. On the road, she finds herself stopping to explore what catches her eye: old, thatched houses, one with an old stove and flowers growing out of the thatch.

One woman saw her looking at her house and invited her in. Another helped her in a downpour to find a B&B so hidden the woman never knew it was in her own town.

She and Jo are now fast friends. Jo has talked with caretakers at medieval abbeys and at the old armory in Kinsale, overlooking the water. She has talked with tours guides, a librarian who told her that more than 5,000 Jews emigrated through Ireland in World War II, a man on a bicycle who recommended the town's Chinese restaurant for dinner.

Ann LaBier savors the memory of Irish food, lamb stew, fresh eggs, blood sausage, fruit breads with sweet butter, strong tea, and the seafood. "The fishermen are out catching what you're eating that night," she said. She had not known her grandparents. She is the youngest in her family, and her grandmother died the year she was born. Her mother's father, she said, came to the U.S. when he was about 14, at the turn of the 20th century. He worked odd jobs, she said, and during Prohibition he ran a speakeasy. Her family has not handed down stories about her grandparents' lives but she thinks about them: about how

"It was breathtaking to be standing on a street with 2,000 people and wondering how many of them were my relatives."

brave they must have been to leave everything they knew and come to a city neighborhood when American businesses used to hang signs outside saying "Irish need not apply." And something of Ireland seems to have come down to her. She has red hair, a Shamrock bracelet and an insistence on respect. And the country draws her back. She remembers how she felt when she stood there for the first time. "It was a sense of the first time you felt like you were home. When we landed," she took a deep breath and let it out slowly, "It felt like where I wanted to be."

After 15 years as a classroom teacher and 23 an administrator in the Bennington Public Schools, Sue Maguire understands the impact of poverty on children. Principal of Mt. Anthony Union High School (MAUHS) since 2002, she's grateful to be in a position that allows her to find and try new solutions for her community.

"If something is good for kids, let's make it happen!" We're sitting in her sunny high school office, its walls celebrating Sue's children's painting and her students' beautiful mosaics. "My job is about giving all kids the same opportunities my children and grandchildren have. Why wouldn't all kids have that?"

MAUHS serves roughly 1,000 students from Bennington, Shaftsbury, Woodford, and Pownal. Its most significant diversity, she reports, is economic. Student population reflects a broad range of household incomes but sixty percent of MAUHS students qualify for free and reduced lunch. Child poverty brings, including hunger, domestic violence, underemployment, inadequate housing, and various unmet physical and mental health needs that interfere with children's learning. When she began wrestling with these troubles for her younger students at Molly Stark, it was logical to reach out. Local agencies and service providers offered help and expertise.

Sue Maguire

by Margot Welch

"I started believing in partnerships when I realized the power they had to help kids. You can often get so much more accomplished working in collaboration rather than isolation."

Since the 1980's, under-resourced schools and civic leaders all around the country have been seeking new ways to meet children's needs. As Sue knows, sharing community resources, funding, services, interns, mentors, enrichment programs and organizational expertise, benefits both schools and their communities. When school days are extended, medical and social work interns support school-based service providers, mentors and volunteers engage with students and their families, everyone learns.

"For me, the community school means access, opportunities for kids who don't have them," she explains. "Kids need multiple pathways to learning. We have many alternative academic programs to help them succeed. We provide a free health clinic, mental health and drug and alcohol counseling, and five full-time tutor mentors [who are] caring, dynamic adults who become part of kids' academic schedules, with the skills and time to see that about 80 students catch up with opportunities. Tutors help all kinds of students with anything they need. There's no single magic bullet: kids are different. It's all important."

Describing only a few of MAUHS' vital school-community partnerships, she referenced its strong relationship with the town's tutorial center, a Bridges program that helps students transition from middle to high school, important connections with the local community college where many, dual-enrolled students take courses and a day and evening

> *"I started believing in partnerships when I realized the power they had to help kids. You can often get so much more accomplished in collaboration rather than isolation."*

program for pupils who are pulling away from school. They take day jobs with local nonprofit and government agencies and receive wages they deposit in local banks. If they miss their evening academic program, they lose the jobs and wages. When bad things happen, students suddenly find themselves homeless, become truant because of difficult home situations, lose access to transportation, or experience devastating, unexpected trauma, Sue and her staff all help, like a family.

Born in Syracuse, New York, Sue attended state schools from kindergarten through graduate school. Her father was a devoted schoolteacher, principal and superintendent and her son is teaching now. Not surprisingly, she plans to mentor new principals when she retires.

"We're influenced by how we grow up. I saw my dad making a huge difference in kids' lives. When I was a child we were never rich, but I always had what I needed and my parents' love. Though our main job is academics, you have to address other parts of kids' lives too and you can't do this without working with the community."

Sue is grateful to have been able to hire people who share her values, her passion, and really care about kids, "But I just set the tone," she says, always modest. "It's the people around me who do all the work. Lots of people care. But some people see barriers. I refuse to believe we can't figure out ways to make things better. What's most meaningful is when a kid in their 30's or 40's approaches me in a store and says, 'Remember me? That time I was all upset and you calmed me down?' or 'Remember when you told me I'd be good at computers?' I may not remember my exact words but these moments always show me how important an educator's job is. Kids will remember the good and the bad. The words we say are so important. Education is a noble profession: I believe that we can make an enormous difference."

♥

Margot Welch and Sue Maguire first met in 1998 at the first of five national conferences Margot ran, at the Harvard Graduate School of Education, about Full Service Community Schools.

Berkshire Morris Men

by Liz Blackshine

With "wintry mix" displayed throughout this month's weather forecast, many Berkshire residents impatiently thaw out and await the warmth and vibrancy that spring promises. Instead of waiting out the cold, this year the local Morris Dance team invites the community to join them in a sacred and joyous pagan May Day ritual of song and dance that beckons all to participate in spring's arrival.

While it may not be true that humans can hurry spring along, the intention of taking part in the waking of the earth from her slumber is an annual ritual many pagan or earth-based cultures have held dear for several centuries before the spread of Christianity.

The term pagan originally referred to a "rustic," "country person," a "peasant" and later it encompassed every religious practice that was not Christian or Jewish. Nicholas VanSant, one of the founding members of the local Morris team, explains, "the pagan piece is the observance of the earth and its cycles. It's not religious in terms of a canon. It is a ritual in that we do it on a regular basis with intention. We don't expect anything magical to happen apart from enriching our lives and enriching the lives of the community which, I think, is enough. We are pagans with a little p." While the Morris dancers of Berkshire County do not necessarily identify with being religiously pagan, they resonate with "being a part of a stream of oral folk tradition passed along directly from one man to another," said Christopher Sblendorio, another of the founding members of the local Morris team.

His interest in the Morris song and dance was sparked in England as he interned at a Rudolf Steiner school. The Berkshire Morris team started in 1982 at Great Barrington Rudolf Steiner School (GBRSS) when Chris was playing a very rare Morris tune in his classroom. Graham Dean, England native, and another longtime staff member of GBRSS was cleaning the halls, passed by Chris's classroom, and danced the precise Morris steps that coincide with the odd tune. Chris and Graham began the now 32-year-old Berkshire Morris dance team, of

Handsworth Longsword Morris Team, 1910 - Photo: English Folk Dance & Song Society

which three of the original six members still remain. Nick, then a parent at the school, said, "I had no idea what it was but as soon as I put the bells on, I knew I wanted to do it! It was special; there was a certain feeling about it that's very dear to me that has grown over time.

At the May Day celebration, you can expect to witness a group of strong jovial men, of varying ages and ethnic backgrounds, dressed in white, red handkerchiefs on their wrists and waist, bells wrapped around their legs, carrying big sticks, and jumping high into the air and around each other in patterns to the music of a diatonic accordion, fiddle, and or the pipe and tabor played by a colorfully dressed, cheerful, beat-keeping melody maker.

Chris often proclaims to the crowd, "the hankies are to attract the audience, the sticks are to wake up the earth out of its winter slumber, and the bells are to attract the fairy folk." He adds that the celebration promotes, "prosperity, good luck, and fertility." Relying heavily on the oral tradition of the folk dance is a unique way of keeping the Morris dance alive and not static.

"We are happy to be a part of a long line of dancers whose rituals made their way to us. And we hope to pass it along to others," said Chris. The dancers take basic moves from one of the basic styles and then add to it.

> "We are happy to be a part of a long line of dancers whose rituals made their way to us. And we hope to pass it along to others."

"We mostly do a tradition called Fieldtown, now this is a Cotswold Morris," says Graham, who got his start at Morris dancing in Shelburne, England, which is in Gloucestershire, also in the Cotswold District. Cotswold District is home to the city where our very own Great Barrington gets its name. Graham continues, "We've created four dances in the Berkshire tradition, which are unique to our team."

At this year's May Day celebration, the team will be dancing one original dance and one traditional dance. Chris said as Nick and Graham strongly agreed, "Somebody's got to do this! We would love for a bunch of young guys to come and take it over from us so we can just sit back, watch and enjoy it."

They concluded, "any men who are crazy enough are welcome to join" them every Monday evening at 7 p.m. at GBRSS for practice. The intrigue is enhanced knowing the Morris dance team starts off every performance season at dawn on May 1, where each year at the same place, they perform for only nature and themselves.

In the 1950s, Jim Davids would come from the Stockbridge Munsee Community Band of Mohican Indians to the Berkshires. He visited with Grace Bidwell, then curator of the Stockbridge Library's Historical Room. In the 1990s, Grace's grandson, Stockbridge Police Chief Richard Wilcox, canoed down the Housatonic River with Davids' son, the Tribal Conservation Officer, whose name is also Jim.

More than 200 years after they left Stockbridge as a group, Mohican people come to the Berkshires to walk in the mountains and to advise in the cleanup of the Housatonic. Sherry White, the Preservation Officer for the Stockbridge Munsee Band of the Mohicans, has an office in Troy, New York and she has a longstanding friendship with Richard.

In conversation with Richard and Barbara Allen, curator of the Stockbridge Historical Collection, Sherry explained that for at least 9,000 years, until the 1600s, the people of the Mohican nation lived along the Muhhuonnut, the waters that are never still—now the Hudson River—and in the lands surrounding it.

"The original Mohican homeland is huge," Richard said, "along both sides of the Hudson River Valley from Vermont to Manhattan an area that included most of Western Massachusetts to the Connecticut River."

> *"The original Mohican homeland is huge, along both sides of the Hudson River Valley [including] most of Western Massachusetts to the Connecticut River."*

Richard's connection to the Mohicans goes back nearly 300 years. His ancestor, Dr. Oliver Partridge, came to Stockbridge in 1771 and served as second physician. The town began as a mission settlement among the Mohicans and people of the Narragansett, Munsee, Delaware, Scatticoke and others, and the English colonists. In Partridge's time, he said, most of the original Stockbridge people had lost their land, but most had not yet left the community.

The Mohicans had moved, under pressure, from Great Barrington to settle in Stockbridge, and they agreed to learn the customs and live by the laws of the Europeans who had often broken covenants with them. It was a difficult choice, Sherry said, and it raised arguments among people who had their own familiar faith, and little reason to trust the colonists.

"Even while we were here, some people did not want to be Christianized," she said. Dr. Oliver Partridge spoke for the Mohicans in the community

Chief Richard Wilcox & Sherry White

by Kate Abbott

and represented their political interests. He treated them when they were ill. He must have sat with them when they were dying. He must have cared for their children. He kept account books, and Richard has read them. Reading the account books give such a vivid sense of Partridge's days, his work, and his concerns, that he feels as though he knows his forbear.

When the Mohicans left Stockbridge, forced to move west, Dr. Partridge agreed to care for the places here they most loved. In 1809, they deeded the Indian Burying Grounds to Oliver and Chief Wilcox is carrying on the work.

"Chief Wilcox has been a friend of the tribe for years," Sherry said. "He has been helpful in keeping the tribe's interest in projects around here. People think because we left here, we have no interest in this place, but we really do." Because she works for the Stockbridge Munsee, she often comes, she said; many of the Stockbridge Munsee do not have the means to travel as she does and to walk in the Ice Glen in October, when the leaves turn colors.

"When people come from Wisconsin to visit, they know: 'If you're going to Stockbridge, find Rick Wilcox,' Sherry said.

Chief Wilcox and Sherry met through her work. Through the years, he said, he has become involved with community preservation and he wanted to make sure whatever he or the town did, they did respectfully.

So Chief Richard Wilcox and Sherry White work together to preserve and care for places important to the people of the Stockbridge Munsee Nation. Three years ago, they cleared and cleaned the stone pillar

Barbara Allen, Chief Richard Wilcox and Sherry White

from the Ice Glen that honors Mohicans who lived and died here. They wanted to keep a balance between restoration and leaving the land in peace, Richard said.

With a preservation grant, they restored the stone staircase and found an Indian head penny embedded in the mortar. Masons would often press a penny into the mortar with the year, he said, to show when they finished the work. The mason who built the stairs left his own memorial token instead. Now, after the cleanup, a visitor can stand near the stone and look down to the river.

"It's great what Rick does," Sherry said. "The Tribe is so grateful, we honored Rick with a blanket. This is significant, a community honor, a sign of strength. We wait for the day when we'll get a blanket."

When they give someone a blanket, they wrap him in it. At Laurel Hill Day on August 25th, Chief Wilcox stood warmly enveloped in his tribute, with Mohican symbols in bright-colored wool.

The Reverend Janet Zimmerman

by Kate Abbott

Originally from Texas, the Reverend Janet Zimmerman worked as a special education teacher for many years before she came to the ministry. She had been teaching at a major university for many years, she said, and then life got quiet for a time, and she could hear and feel another call. A conversation with a friend planted the seed.

"I was talking about what I was longing for and they said, *I thought you came to talk about being a priest.*"

In fact, she had wanted to become a priest as a teenager, but at that time, women were not ordained in the Episcopal Church, she said. Times have changed. She didn't know much about the Northeast until she and her husband came to the southern Berkshires last fall when she became priest-in-charge at a church without walls.

St. George's Episcopal Church in Lee, a congregation 175 years old, decided they could not support both renovations and ministry, she explained. After years of careful conversations, they sold their historic building, she said. They had such a tight community that they wanted to stay together, to focus on programs like the Lee Food Pantry, and not to disperse to other local churches.

Then, St. James Church in Great Barrington, also an Episcopal congregation with long-standing connections in the community, faced the same dilemma. So, the two churches have come together—as people not bound to a place.

Two years ago, they formed Grace Church, and they meet now at Crissey Farm in Great Barrington and keep an office space at 67 State Road

"We come together on Sunday morning and set up church," Zimmerman said. They set up an altar, flowers, chairs and a choir area with a keyboard. On Easter Sunday, they had kites for the kids and strung an umbrella with ribbons, symbolizing their hopes for the earth and creation. Zimmerman said she felt joy on that holiday morning, a sacred celebration, and warmth, and welcome.

> *"With any space, it takes time to feel like a place of worship. People grieve for the loss of beautiful historic buildings. But a church is a community, not a building."*

"With any space, it takes time to feel like a place of worship," she said. "People grieve for the loss of beautiful historic buildings. But a church is a community, not a building. We don't feel restrained. We put our energy into looking out and listening to the needs of the community, learning how we can be of service."

They have found one route to service in the earth in a place they call Gideon's Garden. For the past six years, Dan and Martha Tawczynski, Paul and Keith Tawczynski, and Sue Hayden of Taft Farms in Great Barrington have allowed the congregation to plan and plant two acres of land.

"It's a perfect place for community work," Zimmerman said, "for creation and nurturing. Once the kids grow plants, we share with food banks and community agencies."

Young members of the congregation and volunteers plant the garden, water and care for it all summer and harvest what they grow. They deliver the produce to Breaking Bread Kitchen, the People's Pantry, the Lee Pantry, the Guthrie Center Lunch Program, Habitat for Humanity and more.

Through Gideon's Garden, Zimmerman said, the church has connected with Multicultural Bridge summer camps and families who have come into the community from other countries. Some of these families have taught the church community a great deal about gardening, as they have had gardens in their old or new homes. They also work with the Community Health Program, Railroad Street Youth Project, and Brookside School.

Gideon's Garden also gives seedlings to students at Muddy Brook Elementary School to plant at home. "Young people are affected by this work," Zimmerman said.

Rev. Ted Cobden and Fidel Moreno offered blessings for Gideon's Garden

Taking these partnerships further, the church has held a series of Community Network Dinners. The dinners have led to plans for new services for seniors in need.

We have a responsibility to speak out about people who cannot feed their families, she said, people who need health care, people too often shut out, people who have had experiences different from theirs. She believes God welcomes all people.

That open, welcoming spirit, creativity, and community brought her to Grace Church.

"There's something compelling about this journey," she said, "this willingness to move out into the world." People say, 'When will you build a church.' We are a church. We come together to worship and be fed by the love that never ends, with music and scripture. We welcome guests and visitors, we care for each other. If someone is in need or if someone is isolated or sick, we seek each other out. We make sure people know they are loved and not forgotten."

♥

Celebration

"Everybody can be great...because anybody can serve. You don't have to have a college degree to serve. You don't have to make your subject and verb agree to serve. You only need a heart full of grace. A soul generated by love."

~Reverend Dr. Martin Luther King Jr.

*Celebrating with Music
Rodney Mashia*
Multicultural BRIDGE Facilitator

He remembers the smell of lemon-scented furniture polish. It was a day in spring when his family would open all the windows and rub down the wood, and he would sit with his younger brother, cleaning silver. Family was coming for the holiday, and they cleaned the house. He would help his mother in the kitchen. She made a walnut cake with egg whites to help it rise.

"That is the taste of Passover," said Rabbi Josh Breindel at Temple Anshe Amunim. He remembers homemade macaroons, sparkling apple juice, boiled eggs, and parsley. "I remember the music," he said. As a vocalist now, he loves to share the melodies he knew as a child. Singing to his congregation has power and magic in it. He sings in a clear baritone the  refrain Dayenu it would have been enough. The song exalting that God has given so much more.

"It's rousing," he said, "when the children sing it, everyone claps and stomps." Then, quietly, he sings a psalm he remembers his father singing. It is a song of thanksgiving to God, who turns rocks into pools and flints into fountains. Thinking of the English words for the Hebrew words, he finds himself remembering the translation he grew up with, and he takes a book off the shelf: "What ails thee, oh sea, that thou didst flee, Jordan that thou turns back. Ye mountains that ye skip like a ram..." The answer, he said, is the presence of God. Today, the excitement he feels in preparing for the holiday is almost like the lift of preparing for a vacation.

"I feel the wonder still as an adult," he said. "I want that." This is a holiday caught up in springtime, he said, in renewal, miracles and connection to God. Passover celebrates the Exodus, the day when Moses brought the people of Israel out of Egypt. They have left their slavery and walked into the desert. Everything is new, everything has changed.

"Pesach, Passover, is a festival of freedom," Rabbi Breindel said. He will celebrate with his family, with friends and with his congregation and his city. Temple Anshe Amunim welcomes the community into its Seder on the second night of Passover. They will have a brisket dinner. The Seder is an evening of music and a retelling of the Passover story.

Rabbi Breindel will bring in poetry and share his own stories. Growing up in Providence, R.I., he lived next door to an Egyptian Jewish woman, whose family had fled Egypt in the 1970s. A holiday about freedom contains a call to action, he said. It is easy, even in a glance at the headlines, to find people still fighting to be free.

"It's happening now," he said. "What are we called to do?" Leaders at each table will hold conversations in small groups, to ask questions inspired by the day: "If you had to leave home right now with only what you could carry, what would you bring?" It's a night for students and adults and elders, laughing and singing, he said. And it has moments made for children. At one point in the evening, a child asks the adults to explain parts of the story. Rabbi Breindel remembers asking the four questions as a boy, feeling stage fright as he prepared the words he is now teaching his own students to recognize. And his own 3-year-old son Elijah's turn will come soon. Elijah is looking forward to the holiday, the Rabbi

Rabbi Josh Breindel

by Kate Abbott

said. He is looking forward to seeing his grandmother and searching for Hametz. During Passover, in memory of the people of Egypt and their sudden flight, Jewish families use no leavening, no fermented grains like yeast-risen bread. On the night before the first Seder, the household will search to make sure they have products that are not Kosher for Passover. Traditionally, the search is done by candle light, Rabbi Breindel said. Last year, Elijah got to search with a feather and a flashlight, but this year he will be allowed a candle. Elijah is also looking forward to the search for the Afikoman, a piece of matzah hidden for the children to find.

"It's fun to play with your parents like that," Rabbi Breindel said. The Seder is made to captivate children's imagination and he looksforward to crafting holidays his son will remember. "It's designed to be something for the whole family. You're given a commandment to tell a story [to your children.] It wasn't until I became a dad that some of the richness became clear to me, the idea of passing on this experience.

That's something that touches me deeply." A holiday may be cyclical he said. In some ways, it repeats—the words and the music and the flavors. He and his family will make their own matzah together. He says it tastes much better than the store-bought

> "The Seder is made to captivate children's imaginations. It's designed to be something for the whole family."

kind and is easy to make. And yet the celebration can evolve as his son grows older. A holiday can be new every year, like spring.

♥

Rabbi Josh Breindel was born in New York City and grew up in Providence, RI. He attended Brandeis University, studying philosophy, classics, and law before graduating in 1997. After teaching at Temple Shir Tikvah in Winchester, MA, Rabbi Breindel continued his studies at Hebrew College where he received two Masters in Jewish Studies and Jewish Education. He was ordained at Hebrew College. Rabbi Breindel has been at Temple Anshe Amunim in Pittsfield for five years, and summer is always his busiest season. Many of his congregants are in the Berkshires for the summer, and his congregation increases significantly during this season. This summer in particular was full of joy and celebration for Rabbi. Temple Anshe Amunim celebrated Shabbat Ahavah, Shabbat of Love, and the congregation celebrated all of the love in their lives, parental love, love between siblings, romantic love, and the love of friendship. He also published two pieces for JewishBoston.com on the subjects of Jewish science fiction and comics or graphic novels for Judaism. The biggest celebration this summer for Rabbi Breindel was his mother's Bat Mitzvah, where he called his mother to read from the Torah for the first time.

George & Irinia Cami

by Siobhan Connally

George Cami remembers the feeling of Easter joy as a child growing up in Greece—the music, the dancing, the snitching of meat from the roasting lamb. Cami, the owner of Aegean Breeze in Great Barrington has lived in the Berkshires since he opened the restaurant with a business partner in 2001, three years after coming to America from Corfu, a Greek island in the Ionian Sea. The way he sees it, America is still the land of opportunity. "We come for the children. Opportunity is better here. Good schools. Life is better here," he said. Even in the work of food, Cami sees opportunity. "There is more healthy food in the U.S., more vegetarian food. More local organic produce. In Greece, these things are limited."

In many ways, George doesn't miss his homeland. He has his family; he sees his relatives frequently, and they are able to keep fundamental traditions alive here, both in business and at home. "My father raised bees, and my grandfather raised bees, so I raise bees," George said, laughing. "Kids love the honey, and it's better than sugar." He also gets the opportunity to celebrate two Easters—Roman Catholic Easter and Eastern Orthodox Easter. Although Easter is universal in that it commemorates the death and resurrection of Christ as conveyed in the Bible, in the Greek tradition it is observed in a slightly different way, without the secular encroachment of magical bunnies and baskets filled with sugary candies.

It begins with 40 days of Lent, where the faithful eat an all-vegetarian diet and ends in a day-long celebration of feasting, music, dancing and merriment. Every city in Greece has different traditions, he said. In Corfu, the celebration of Easter (Pascha) is a weeklong event that begins on Palm Sunday, the Sunday before Easter.

On Good Monday, Corfiots begin preparations. They shop, and they bake traditional Easter breads called tsoureki. Tsoureki is a sweet, braided yeast bread with citrusy flavors. Religious services, hymns, candle-lighting and the ringing of bells usher in different traditional celebrations during the next few days of Holy Week. The first bell instructs the residents to start dying the traditional red Easter eggs, a custom that symbolizes rebirth and nature. Bells on the morning of Good Friday call the faithful to church, where they commemorate Christ's descent from the cross. Choruses and bands perform through the day and night in a kind of funereal observation.

On the Saturday preceding Easter, the faithful gather at their church for a re-enactment of the earthquake that followed Christ's resurrection. As the appointed time arrives (11 a.m.) bells sound, people proclaim to each other

"Christos Anesti" to each other (Christ has risen) and respond, "Alithos Anesti," (He has truly risen) amid the clamor of bands parading through the streets and people tossing clay pots and vases from windows and balconies, so they noisily crash onto the streets below. A slaughtered lamb is slow roasted on a spit for the next day's feast. At midnight, a Christian Mass is celebrated, which marks the resurrection of Christ and ushers in Pascha.

First, the 40-day Lenten fast is broken with Mayiritsa, a traditional Easter soup that is made of lamb and offal (cleaned intestines and other organ meats) as well as scallions and rice. "We don't use organ meats at the restaurant," George said explaining the Easter soup he serves patrons. Traditional flavors and American sensibilities don't always mix: "People are healthier here. They don't want the fatty meats."

In America, Greek Easter is more of a family affair. George's relatives take turns hosting Easter celebrations and Holy Week events are condensed into one, eight-hour celebration of food and family. "We spend seven or eight hours at the table singing, dancing," he said, "the more people the merrier."

Greek Easter at the restaurant, however, is a little more formal. It mixes Greek traditions with an American flavor. The first of these arrive in the form of hard-boiled eggs dyed a festive red. George hand-dyes 200 eggs, which he serves at the table in place of the usual olives and pita offerings. The custom is to crack the eggs as one would clink a glass during a toast and the egg that doesn't break brings the bearer good luck. Over time, George has noticed at his restaurant that more and more people are gravitating toward more traditional Greek foods, especially at Easter. "For (Roman Catholic) Easter we had lamb and ham," George said. "We sold only four orders of ham."

♥

George Cami was born in a small village in Greece, and began his cooking career there. He moved to the United States and his large family joined him here. He and his wife, Irinia, opened Aegean Breeze in 2001, and they have lived in Great Barrington for the past 14 years. His family helps in the restaurant, including his two children who go to Monument Mountain High School. He plans to continue with the restaurant as well as expanding into catering. This article about Easter dinners at Aegean Breeze brought several people to this unique event.

"We spend seven or eight hours at the table singing, dancing, the more people, the merrier."

Gabriela Cruz, Maria Soria & Lucia Quizhpi

by Kate Abbott

A political rebel sits against a tree in an olive orchard in Jerusalem. He knows he is hunted. He has spoken out in the streets. This is a tense time. An imperial power on one side and a party of religious conservatives on another find him a threat because he tells people they are people. Around him in the darkness, his companions have fallen asleep among the tree roots. He knows the soldiers will find him. This is his last night. He stays awake alone, scuffing the soft dust, watching the moon between dry branches, and thinking of the flashing warmth, the aliveness that comes when he holds a sick man or speaks to an audience and feels them listening.

Tonight, across the world, people will remember this story. This is Maundy Thursday, the holiday of the last supper. It is the fifth day of La Semana Santa, or Holy Week, leading to Easter Sunday. And across Central and South America, whole communities will re-create Jesus' vigil in the garden of Gethsemane, Cerro de Los Olivos, on the night before he died.

Gabriela Cruz from Oaxaca, Mexico, Maria Soria from Ambato, Ecuador, and Lucia Quizhpi from Deleg, Ecuador, came to Multicultural BRIDGE in Housatonic to talk about what La Semana Santa is like in the places where they were born. Maria lives in Lee now, Lucia in Great Barrington and Gabriela in Sheffield. BRIDGE Executive Director Gwendolyn Hampton VanSant translated as they explained in Spanish.

"People go to church every night to pray," Gabriela said. It is a time of respect and peace, she said. People do not dance or listen to music; they

Gabriela Cruz of BRIDGE with Award winning "Frontline" correspondent Maria Hinojosa

don't fight or watch television. Families gather and make meals that take days. In Mexico, Gabriela's family served a shrimp cake with cactus and potatoes. In Ecuador, they make a soup, La Fanesca, with 12 kinds of beans and seeds—lentils, hominy, lupin seed, garbanzo beans and more, representing the 12 apostles, and also bacalao, dried smoked codfish. It takes a long time to make because they soak some grains for several days, Maria said. For dessert, they cook down ripe figs with brown sugar and cinnamon and serve them with cheese. "It is a beautiful time," Gabriela said. The family comes together, from the grandparents to the youngest grandchild. People take time to reflect on their lives.

They are living the story. From Jesus' arrival in Jerusalem, on Palm Sunday, through Judas' betrayal, to Jesus' capture and public execution, they play the scenes and feel the tension, the grief and the relief in them. In Lucia's small village, people dress like soldiers. A group of carefully chosen men are the apostles, Los Santos Varones, dressed in white and wearing crowns. A man who acts as Jesus carries the cross in procession, and the soldiers cuff him to it.

"It is very real," she said. "It's more than a pageant." The actors are chosen a year ahead, and it is an honor. "They do it happily," she said. Tonight in Oaxaca, the priest leads a re-enactment of the last supper. Twelve men play

Maria Soria, Rocio Chevez, Patricia Cambi of the BRIDGE Women to Women Program

the apostles. And the priest washes their feet, as Jesus washed his friends' feet that night in the New Testament.

On Friday morning, Gabriela said, the whole town goes to church. Families bring images of Jesus and the Virgin Mary from home. They parade through the streets on carpets of brightly colored designs in flower petals, colored sand, and wood dust. They visit the prisons to talk with prisoners. And in the afternoon, they re-enact the death and burial of Jesus. At night, after Mass, they cleanse the streets with water.

In Ecuador, Saturday is a day of silence, hope and waiting, Maria said. The church covers images of Jesus with cloth, and Saturday is an all-night vigil, waiting for the resurrection. And on Sunday, they celebrate. In the Berkshires, Maria spends the holiday with her sister; they get as many of the grains as they can and make La Fanesca.

Here the celebration of la Semana Santa doesn't exist, Gabriela said. Her family goes to church on Palm Sunday and on Easter because there are no other celebrations. In their countries, this week is a holiday, and shops and government services close at least on Friday and Saturday. Here it is hard, they said because they have to work.

"Today, in these days we live in, a lot of people forget the significance of Holy Week," Maria said. "It becomes a diversion, a trip, when we should dedicate ourselves to prayer and reflection." In a foreign land like this, she said, through religion and culture people maintain unity. Here, El Señor Romero Guerrero of Pittsfield helps them to keep their faith, Maria said. Though not a priest, he has studied, and he helps with communions and baptisms. They preserve what they can. And Lucia, telling her stories, preserves the processions through the village she left at 18; Maria and Gabriela came from cities, but Lucia's home village no longer exists. Everyone has immigrated to the United States or died, she said.

"Lamentably, I lived this religion as a child," she said. She too feels distanced from it here. As a mother, she pushes for a connection to that faith and that experience, she said, but her children are missing it. Lucia's daughter sat beside her, listening. And the evening ended with a warm bowl of La Fenesca in a dish patterned with sunflowers.

> "...in these days we live in, a lot of people forget the significance of Holy Week."

In the year 1909, William Howard Taft was America's 27th President, the American flag sported only 45 stars and sugar cost a mere four cents a pound. It was a time before the invention of zippers, Band-Aids, traffic lights, penicillin or bubble gum, and it was also the year Minnie Gertrude Golden was born.

I sit across from Stephanie Wright, one of Minnie's oldest granddaughters. I listen raptly to stories of her large, tightly knit family and am awed that I have stumbled across a branch of one of the oldest African American family trees in Berkshire County. Stephanie's family roots trace back to 1855 when Sam Golden, her great grandfather, moved from Fishkill, New York, to begin a farming life in Sheffield. Sam's grandson, Cornelius Golden Jr., met and married Minnie.

When Minnie and Cornelius married in 1928, it was a controversy. They went through trying times as a mixed raced couple raising bi-racial children in the early '30s and '40s.

> "Gram loved her family, she loved having us all around her..."

"Poppy and Gram met in Norwalk, Connecticut. He met her and refused to return home to Sheffield without her. He was a very convincing man," Stephanie said. "Sometimes [their life together] got tough, but they always made it through. My grandparents were hard workers. They never gave up."

Minnie worked for Dr. Steven A. Moore as a nanny and housekeeper until age 85. Cornelius worked as a carpenter to help construct the Mid-Hudson bridge in Poughkeepsie, New York, and with his own construction company he built many homes in Sheffield that still stand to this day.

"Popi was a man of average height," Stephanie said, "but I remember Gram being a tall, stately woman [in her early years]. It was when Gram retired that our relationship became stronger. I visited her nearly every day. We would talk about anything and everything. She was very news-conscious. She had an opinion on everything, and she wanted to know your opinion too. Gram was a hot ticket until the day she died." Stephanie smiled as she recounted the years of Minnie's long life.

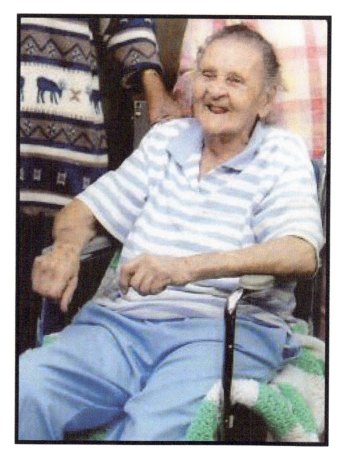

Minnie and Cornelius had been married for 48 years when Cornelius died in 1974. They had eight children and those children have produced a legion of grandchildren, great-grandchildren, great-great-grandchildren and even a few great-great-great grandchildren.

"Gram loved her family," Stephanie said. "She loved having us all around her every chance she could get. She kept us together. Family was important to Gram, and it's still important to all of us. We just love each other so much, and

I am so thankful for that." Stephanie's family was the driving force behind her success when she moved from North Carolina to Berkshire County.

"Mom was born in Great Barrington, but she married my father, who was from the south and moved there," she said. "I spent most of my elementary school years in segregated North Carolina. My family moved back to the Berkshires when I was in fifth grade. I attended high school at Mount Everett Regional, [a predominately white school]. "It was the height of the Civil Rights Movement back then. The South was in flames, people were killing and fighting over race, but I was clueless here. I had so many cousins at school, some with blond hair and blue eyes, but they loved us and were proud of us, and [the tension in the rest of the country] didn't seem to touch us. My family made my experience in high school fun."

Perhaps it is Minnie's strength that continues to keep their family close to this very day. "Gram was a very strong person," Stephanie said. "She always wanted things to be fair and straight. If she ever had a problem, she went right to the source, and she wouldn't leave until the problem got solved. She taught me to not only speak up when things are bothering me but to speak up and applaud the good in the world too." Many have described Minnie Golden as a wonderful woman. She grew to love her home in Sheffield and became a treasured and respected member of her community. When asked what she remembered most about her grandmother, Stephanie was moved to tears. "She believed that an apple a day kept the doctor away," she said. "She also raised her own chickens and maintained her own gardens. Now that I reflect on her, I realize that she believed in excellence. She pursued excellence, expected excellence and showered excellence upon us."

Minnie was 100 years old when Stephanie pulled out an old tape recorder and captured her reciting from memory "Come Little Leaves," a poem by George Cooper. On the tape, Minnie's strong, rhythmic voice speaks these words.

"Cricket, goodbye, we've been friends so long. Little brook, sing us your farewell song. Say you are sorry to see us go. Ah! You are sorry, Right well, we know."

Minnie's life began on Feb. 11 in Sharon, Connecticut, and came to a sweet conclusion in Sheffield, at Fairview Commons Nursing Home, just a few months before her 105th birthday. This may seem like the end, but Minnie's story will continue to live on in her family and in her beloved home.

♥

In Loving Memory of Minnie Golden

Minnie Golden & Stephanie Wright

by Nik Davies

Living within the majestic view of Berkshire County, many hold dear a set of hills or mountains in the region. The familiar mountains seem to reflect on Martin Luther King Jr.'s last speech in April 1968, often referred to as the "mountaintop speech." Dr. King eloquently and passionately relays a vision of gazing out over a mountaintop and beholding his dreams. Imagine the great soul of Martin Luther King Jr. looking out over our local mountain landscape and seeing Berkshire youth giving shape to his vision of social and economic equality. He might see youth leaders speak at the upcoming 14th annual Interfaith celebration of the Martin Luther King Jr. National Holiday.

If King gazed over Mount Greylock, he might see Mount Greylock High School senior, Crystal Haynes, called into the principal's office for her exemplary skillful conduct in cultural conflict resolution. With years of experience as a Youth Leader in Multicultural BRIDGE Youth Corps, Crystal has great confidence in helping her student peers peacefully and constructively resolve situations involving racial prejudice and stereotypes.

As Dr. King taught, "you need to try to get a sense of understanding from each side," she said. Crystal became involved with Multicultural BRIDGE Youth Corps three years ago when the organization responded to a request from Mount Greylock High School. They offered a school-wide series of workshops to collaboratively build a new sense of community. As a result, Crystal said, "there were big changes in the faculty. I could tell they really cared and made an effort to welcome new people. Our school is making big strides for the community."

Crystal resides in the Greylock ABC House, which welcomes young scholars from around the country and supports them in the Berkshires. As an African American originally from Brooklyn, New York, Crystal has bravely addressed ignorant comments and even hateful remarks. When she faces these kinds of challenges, she said, she "looks to King as the ultimate example of courage and strength, the definition of peace." As she has courageously taken on racial integration, not only has she become a part of the community in Williamstown, she has also stepped into leadership with much grace and success. She was recently inducted into the Governor's Youth Council. There she represents Berkshire County's youth, working for their needs on a state level. While racial integration was an enormous contribution Dr. King made to the nation, he wrote in his book, *Strength to Love*: "Desegregation is only a partial, though necessary, step towards the final goal which we seek to realize genuine intergroup and interpersonal living."

> "You need to try to get a sense of understanding from each side."

Crystal Haynes, Will Conklin & Austen Dupont

by Liz Blackshine

This genuine, inter-group living resonates with local youth leader and Program Director of Greenagers, Will Conklin.

Glancing over Monument Mountain, Dr. King, in his vision, might see Mr. Conklin leading a group of teenagers of various economic backgrounds to create gardens, clear trails, become stewards of the earth and their community. Greenagers programs include education, activism, community service, as well as making it a priority to pay youth for their contributions to the community. "Anytime [we're] talking about economics and community building, creating a resilient local economy, if [we're] not engaging young people in that community, then [we're] perpetuating a stagnant system," Will said. "The income gaps are as important as racial gaps." Among other groups, Will reaches out to school guidance counselors to recruit youth of diverse backgrounds. He refers to Martin Luther King Jr. as making our nation a richer place to live. He defined that richness as "talking to people from different backgrounds on a one-to-one, equal level, and asking the hard questions."

If Dr. King, in his visioning on the mountaintop, had a glimpse of Mount Everett and East Mountain, he might see the articulate high school senior Austen DuPont, a Youth Operational Board Leader of Railroad Street Youth Project (RSYP) asking hard questions about economic and social inequalities. Austen points to segregation between income classes at his high school, as well as aspects of the curriculum based around assumptions of financial wealth. At RSYP, youth of all backgrounds are "encouraged to have a voice, and are welcome to use the place as an actual resource," Austen explained. Among other activities, he and fellow RSYP participants head once a month to briefing sessions at the United Nations to lift their voices with concern and suggestions for international issues. When asked about the importance of celebrating MLK Jr. Day in Berkshire County, Austen responded enthusiastically, "This holiday is like Thanksgiving for Martin Luther King!"

♥

Crystal with BRIDGE Director Gwendolyn Hampton VanSant

Beginning her 17th year as educational director at Hevreh of the Southern Berkshires as well as being in the midst of the High Holy days, Paula Hellman is a busy woman. There are new families to meet and new educational programs to administer. Yet even as the temple is transforming—windows removed and a tent erected temporarily—to accommodate the nearly 700 worshippers who come to celebrate Rosh Hashanah and Yom Kippur, it's all part of an invigorating cycle for Hevreh, which is also celebrating its 13th year at its State Road location. Still, she's never too busy to tell a story.

"I find that everything is a story," laughs Paula, who often encounters herself on a tiny chair amid tiny scholars, telling tales from the Old Testament. One of her favorites is of Abraham in the desert.

"He's with Sarah, and the tent flaps are up so he could welcome visitors. He runs to greet them. Washes their feet. Runs to get a cow to make them dinner. We learn that not only is this an obligation, but that this is a good thing for them to do. To welcome guests. To feed guests." It is an illustration that is also reminiscent of the Jewish harvest festival – Sukkot, a seven-day observance that literally means Feast of Booths and is traditionally held five days after Yom Kippur.

"(It) is a time of great rejoicing," notes Paula. "Traditionally, when we were an agricultural society, families would literally move into the fields, erecting a temporary dwelling called a Sukkah or a booth, and they would live there while they were doing the harvest."

As a remembrance of that time, many families still build the three-sided, roofless structures in their yards that house a table laden with the bounty of harvest. She explains the Sukkah at Hevreh is decorated each year by the children, using gourds, flowers, fruits, and tree boughs. The three walls are wrapped in twine and woven with corn stalks.

"It is a beautiful thing: It has no solid roof so that you can look up and see the stars and traditionally, it has an open wall so that you can see people coming and welcome them.

"One of the traditions of the holiday is that you wave something called a lulav and an etrog. Lulav is made up of three things: myrtle

> "...when we were an agricultural society, families would move into the fields, erecting temporary dwellings called Sukkah..."

Paula with Gwendolyn

leaves, which represent the eyes; palm branch, which represents the spine; and a willow branch which represents the lips. And the Etrog is another name for a citron, that has a sweet scent and a strong taste and represents the heart. When held together they represent essentially your whole self. Waved in all directions North, South, East, West, up, down…so that that we have a sense of connecting totally in a totality with God." And as Holy Days come to a close, they do so with Simchat Torah, which means Joy of the Torah and the scrolls are unrolled in the synagogue.

"It emphasizes that we are in a cycle, going from the end to the beginning. In this ceremony students who have a bar or bat mitzvah in 2013 will receive the Torah portion they will read for the first time. "After that ceremony we roll up the Torahs, put on the Torah covers and we dance." Which reminds her of another story.

"Arthur Waskow, in his book 'Season of Our Joy,' he talks about Rosh (meaning head) Hashanah as how we worship God in our intellect. Yom

Paula Hellman

Siobhan Connally

Kippur, which is fasting, strains the heart. Sukkot, as harvest, makes us think in terms of gathering with hands and Simchat Torah is the dance. "Head, heart hands, and feet … the whole living intuit becomes part of what we do at High Holy Season. And in our school we try to convey that joy. Through stories. Getting the children to have a sense that they are creating a community and continuing that into the world.

"We teach at our school it's up to us to have a relationship with God and to understand that we are responsible to take care of the planet and heal the rifts within our community. That's one of the things we try to convey to our children."

♥

Paula Hellman was born and raised on the Upper West Side of Manhattan. After graduating from Bronx High School of Science and NYU, she worked as a vocational guidance counselor in Brooklyn. After being a part of the Temple Anshe Amunim congregation in Pittsfield, she learned of Hevreh, which was closer to her home. The congregation was just starting, and they were hiring a Religious School Director. Paula began working in that position when the school had only 26 students. At the time of her retirement in June 2014, the religious school had more than 130 students. It was important to her to be involved in the religious community and to make a difference in peoples' lives through education. Now, Paula is enjoying her retirement by taking walks and traveling with her husband.

Bill & Steve Robinson

by Roberta Dews

Whenever one of Catherine Robinson's children came to her with a special request, something they were especially passionate about, she would acquiesce. Catherine, who passed away at the age of 81, saw in her children's desires something that went beyond the surface.

"I always remembered that we would discuss buying something for them, and no matter how high the cost, she would get it," said Bill Robinson, thinking of his wife's efforts.

On the day I visited Bill and his son, Steve, at their sprawling 200-acre Sunny Banks Ranch in Becket, Massachusetts, the sky was overcast, with a bit of chill in the air. Clad in thick rubber boots, jeans and a plaid shirt, Steve, who was outside working near the stables, looked every bit the part of a cowboy.

Today, that is, in fact, who he is. After retiring as a firefighter in New Haven, Connecticut, Steve is a full-time professional cowboy and horse trainer. The stables at Sunny Banks are filled with horses. Steve's great-grandfather on his dad's side bought the ranch for $900 in 1906, and since then it has never left the family's control. It has become not only a place where Steve's love of horses can take center stage through rodeos, clinics and trail rides offered to the public, but for a time, it has also served as a refuge for young people who've encountered difficulties and challenges in their lives. Perhaps, this is the vision that Catherine saw of her son before he could fully imagine the possibilities.

"When I was a baby, I would get excited when I saw a horse. [When I was a child], everybody wanted to play army and I wanted to play cowboys and Indians. The cowboys from TV became my heroes," Steve said. "My mother was the facilitator of our dreams. She bought my brother and me saddles. We didn't even have horses at the time." But Catherine was a woman who not only envisioned who her children could be but also had a vision of who she could be as well, despite a society that encouraged women to stay in the home.

"My mom started the Tiny Tots program in New Haven; she was a licensed practical nurse, an educator on several academic boards, and one of her best friends was Joseph Liebermann," Steve said. "I remember (Liebermann) sitting in my house when my mother was running for alderwoman. She was a feminist. For a Black woman to be a feminist, there were many lines to cross over." She became an alderwoman and the first person of color to serve on the board of the Community Foundation

Steve Robinson at Sunny Banks Ranch

of Greater New Haven. She was later invited by President Lyndon B. Johnson to come to Washington, D.C. for a civil rights event, Bill said. Bill attributed his wife's many accomplishments to one thing: her character.

"At the time, there was a big clamor about inequality in the northern schools. At that time, in the late '50s and '60s, when they had the riots, that was a big change for all of us," Bill said. "I think things just happened and she was there. She saw a need, and she did it." And Bill helped to facilitate her vision as well.

"A lot of times she'd have to go away and yes, I took care of the kids. I was a policeman and worked the midnight shift," said Bill, who also received help from Catherine's nearby family. "We made it work; we never left our kids alone."

Indeed, Catherine set such a strong example that the legacy of her actions continues to reverberate with Steve today. Inspired by her, he wants to move Sunny Banks in a new direction. In the midst of a tight economy, Steve still wants to provide offerings to those seeking his services; however, he wishes to devote his time to one group, in particular. "I have championships in the rodeo associations I'm in, but God wants me to stay (here); this is a gift," Steve said. "Going forward, I want to take some kids who need mentoring or those going into programs, and bring them to the farm. It's a better chance to put this in their system than jail."

Bill and Steve Robinson

> "When I was a baby, I would get excited when I saw a horse. [As a child] everybody wanted to play army and I wanted to play Cowboys and Indians."

♥

In Loving Memory of Catherine Robinson

Photo from The Dramatic Guild of America

R esilience is the ability to convert the negative to a positive. Sometimes, out of the darkest, most devastating challenges and catastrophes come beauty and new beginnings. For Yvette "Jamuna" Sirker, challenges including a catastrophic hurricane have led to a full life in the Berkshires, changing the lives of the young people at Reid Middle School every year.

Jamuna received her MFA in theater from New York University. When she went in search of acting roles, she said, it was one of the first times she had truly encountered racism. She has played Lady Macbeth and other theater, television and film roles, but often the only roles she could find were for maids or mistresses, and she was turned away for other parts.

"There were simply no roles for people of color; it was truly heartbreaking," she said. "So I realized I had to create those roles."

She set out on a new mission: to give voice to underrepresented people in theater. She wrote a play set in the Mississippi Flood of 1927 from the perspective of the people it affected. She found she loved writing. She found a passion.

But like many artists living in New York City, she felt something was missing. She was drawn to the Berkshires by Kripalu in Stockbridge. She began teaching yoga there, and she received her Sanskrit name, Jamuna.

"There was something magical, a healing quality in the earth in this area," She said. "I felt a connection to this place."

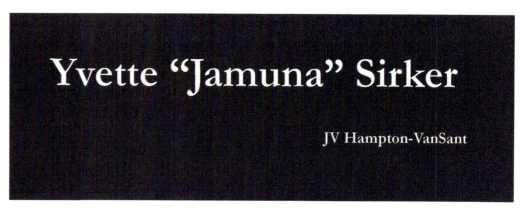

Yvette "Jamuna" Sirker

JV Hampton-VanSant

When she finished her MFA, she felt as though "everything needed to stop" so she could reconnect, she said. The day she graduated, she walked the 80 blocks from Juilliard to the West Village. She happened on the Sweet Basil jazz club and got some of the best advice of her life from an old high school compatriot—internationally known jazz musician Wynton Marsalis.

"[Wynton] said to me, *Go home. Go back to New Orleans for a while and get your soul back*," she said.

So she returned to New Orleans, to Louisiana and found a new love: teaching. She taught in public schools, as well as at Tulane University and Dillard University. She realized teaching yoga had given her skills in honoring people and working with different ways of learning.

"Rudy Peirce, an excellent Kripalu yoga teacher, told me once, *It's not your job ever to decide whether or not someone will be good at something. Your job is to honor their soul and honor their journey, and plant seeds of hope. That is your job as a teacher*," she said.

She worked in theater in New Orleans as she had in New York, directing and writing plays and building a network for local actors, creating roles for actors of color and giving directors a place to meet local performers.

Shortly before the largest catastrophe of her life, she wrote *Pink Collar Crime*, a play revolving around the oil industry's role in destroying Louisiana wetlands.

Three months after the theater went to press announcing *Pink Collar Crime* coming out, in August of 2005, Hurricane Katrina struck and decimated New Orleans. The theater sustained heavy damage, and the play ran nine months after Katrina to sold-out houses in a makeshift community center turned theater. It received national and international coverage. When Katrina hit, Jamuna was tenured faculty in the New Orleans Public School system. She was teaching acting, dance and creative writing to students in second grade through 12th grade. She lost her job when 100 of the 127 public schools closed and her department, Talented in the Arts, did not re-open. Jamuna became one of the thousands of tenured faculty let go from Louisiana schools.

Yvette Jamuna Sirker appears in "When the Sky Falls"

"Suddenly I was homeless," she said. "I was a refugee. People would tell me that I was an 'evacuee.' But that wasn't true. Evacuees have something to come back to. I lost everything."

But she had more than many did, she said. She had enough to move and start over. An artist relief effort came through for her. She received artist residencies, which gave her a place to lay her head at night and continue creating.

She wrote *When The Sky Falls* in this changing time. Because of her work as an artist, she had to be close to New York, she said, but she did not want to return to the city. She came to the Berkshires and has lived here ever since.

In recent years, she has worked with the youth at Reid Middle School as a writing and reading specialist. She sees roughly 150 students in a semester and she always gives them a final group project: to produce a talk show, to write, edit and film it and air it on local television.

"When you give students the opportunity to make something that matters to them, they put their hearts and souls into it," she said. "They don't always understand exactly how much they are learning, and that is the beauty of arts integration with Common Core standards."

She also continues to write and direct. This month, she served as artistic director for *10 Shorts* at the Whitney Center for the Arts in the annual 10x10 Upstreet Festival in Pittsfield. She put together *10 Shorts* with work from local performers, many of them women of color, and her own work.

"There was a hunger for this kind of art," she said. "People came up to me after and told me how much they appreciated it, saying that now they knew what they had been missing."

> *"There were simply no roles for people of color; it was truly heartbreaking. So I realized I had to create those roles."*

She hopes now to work in theater in the Berkshires as she has in New Orleans. Her work here in writing, teaching, and directing goes on. After a hurricane can come a rainbow—out of tragedy can come art, beauty, and meaning.

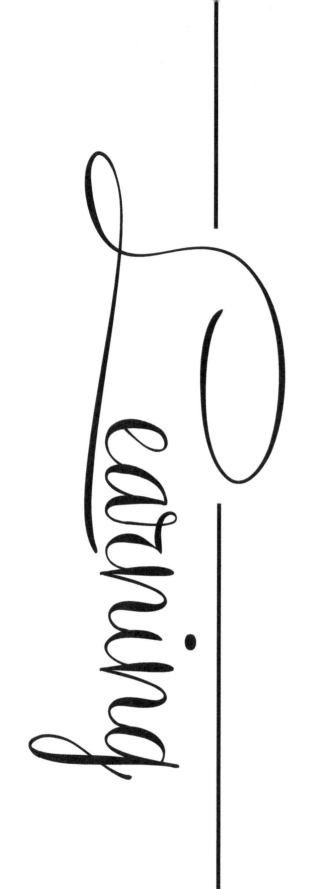

"True learning is the ability to decide upon change and then follow through with clear mind and steady purpose. True learning is the ability to take action."

~Richard Heckler-Strozzi

Connecting through Learning
Dr. Rasool with granddaughter
Lenox Memorial Middle & High School

Asma Abbas talks about her life and experience in many ways, in philosophy and theory and listening silence. People often ask someone who has suffered to tell a story, Abbas explains, only in the way they want to hear it. She remembers giving a talk and saying she felt thankful for fellowships that have helped her, and people afterward saying, 'I can't believe how much you have struggled', and they knew nothing about her life, her family or the advantages she has also had.

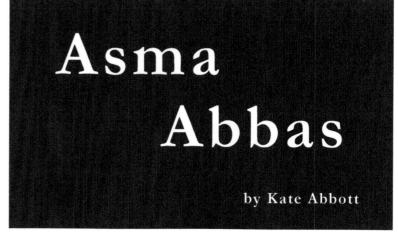

Asma Abbas

by Kate Abbott

"Why should I tell you a story you already know?" she said. "Why does someone have to tell a story in first person about my suffering, my background?"

She brings passionate curiosity to understanding the stories of others, to her research and her classrooms. Abbas has taught politics and philosophy at Bard College at Simon's Rock for ten years, more than four as Chair in the Division of Social Studies. She is researching the politics of love on the verges.

She is studying people at the boundaries, on the edges of societies, and the ways people believe in God and love their parents and their children, their country—and what they feel is worth suffering or dying for.

"There has to be a different way of understanding what people who are suffering do," she said. "People relate to pain differently. My experience in coming from Pakistan, from a background of labor activists, is not focused on how suffering will end."

She came from Karachi to the New School to Pennsylvania State University and now to the Southern Berkshires to teach college classes. She published a book, "Liberalism and Human Suffering, in 2010.

In her teaching, she draws on a wide range of writers, scholars, playwrights and philosophers—Jean-Jacques Rousseau, Jean Rhys' Wide Sargasso Sea, Ingeborg Bachmann, Assia Djebar, Tony Kushner, Horatio Alger, Malcolm X and more.

She wants to teach her students to question, she said, to feel they belong in any conversation and to affirm that they are there to struggle with ideas—and the struggle is exhilarating.

Many of her students have welcomed the challenge to engage in any deeply theoretical exercise, she said. But she finds herself worried by some students, by a resistance to thinking. They want to study what speaks to them, she said—but how will they know what speaks to them unless they experiment, push themselves, and look for new thoughts and responses and arguments?

"Isn't a way of being hospitable a way of telling a story?"

She recalls moments of tension in a class when students study something new to them. When she asks them to open themselves to new ideas, she may also make herself vulnerable, she said. She takes a risk, hoping they will recognize it and take one, too.

She hopes they will claim a space for themselves even when others say it is not theirs. She has had students read

W.E.B. DuBois next to Rousseau and think about what happens when people who have no place stand up to claim it. When the world defines someone as a problem, how effective can they be in any change they work for?

"We have to change the problems," she said.

She studies what moves her and what she wants to change. And she finds power in the idea that one person can change the structure, the society around her, even the state.

"Politics is the capacity to make meaning," she said. "How do you do that if you shut out thought?"

When a state has power over someone's life, political thought can touch the most private places. And people who protest may suffer.

"When we have to fix the world and have nothing to fix it with, we fix it with everything we've got," she said. "It's like hospitality with nothing, being the outsider and the host all the time...trying to invite people to think."

Professor Abbas with her daughter

This kind of experience is a common one. She has often talked recently with professionals, people of color who have come back to pursue advanced degrees in their mature years. Many were told as young students, "You go back and fix up your neighborhoods, because no one else will"—and they did. But they look back now and see that they were working with someone else's ideas. Now they want to claim their place among the thinkers.

"For people who are suffering, the moments they're made to feel included are on the terms of others," she said.

She sets her own terms. She may explore them in political theory or in a quiet invitation to listen and to talk.

"Isn't a way of being hospitable a way of telling a story?" she said.

It is too easy to deny someone's suffering "or find something redeeming in it—you are the meek who will inherit the earth—and both are ways of not thinking about what someone is actually doing," she said.

Denying the people also denies the causes of pain. "Violence is not abstract or invisible," she said. But political language can try to make it so. "We give [terror] a sense of otherness that keeps it distant and us uninvolved ' she wrote in In Terror, in Love and out of Time, an essay in the anthology At the Limits of Justice: Women of Color on Terror in 2014.

So how can thought and language change, so anyone can see suffering and people who suffer, close and involved? She asks the question in her books, in conversations with her students and in TEDx talks at UC Berkeley.

She wants a world open to people who live with pain and survive, and love.

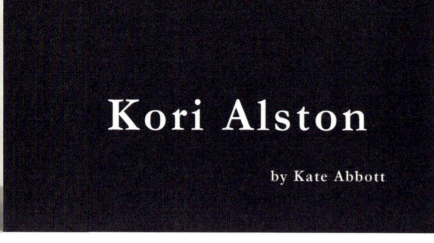

Kori Alston

by Kate Abbott

In the final production of *Henry V* at Shakespeare & Company this summer, Kori Alston of Housatonic, in the role of Henry, spoke to his men before the battle of Agincourt. "We few, we happy few, we band of brothers for he today that sheds his blood with me shall be my brother." Some 8,500 battered campaigners, mostly longbowmen, waited on an October morning to face 50,000 French troops.

"In the final show, doing that speech, some of my soldiers were in tears, and it was genuine," he said. "I felt my heart breaking. I realized they weren't crying just for their own lives but for my life. It hit me for the first time that I was going to die as well." He had struggled with Henry's character in rehearsal, he said, and with this famous speech.

"The biggest challenge was understanding why he would go on with only one-tenth of the men the French had.

And all his men were sick," he said. "I wanted to find the Henry in me. I believed him to be a good guy at heart. How could he push on with these men who were dying, because some document written 200 years ago said he should be the king of France?" Then he began to look closely at Henry's conversations. And he began to find the boy and the man behind the soldier.

"I was working through the feeling that you're worthless and you're supposed to represent everyone. People treat you like you're a child, and you're supposed to be the king of England," he said, not just a king, but powerful among kings. This past summer, Kori was one of twelve students in Shakespeare & Company's, Shakespeare & Young Company. He spent the intense nine-week program learning the subtleties of text and characters, combat, voice work and movement.

He spoke about his love of acting and of writing while he was home on Thanksgiving break from the Walnut Hill School for the Performing Arts in Natick, where he is now in his second year. He had just closed a production of John Guare's "Six Degrees of Separation." He fell in love with theater, he said, as a young student at the Rudolph Steiner School. There, everyone had to act, and in first grade he had his first part. He was a shy and nervous kid, he said, but when he walked onto the stage, his shyness fell away. After that, he tried out for any play he could, for leading roles. In his freshman year at Monument Mountain Regional High School, he took an acting and directing class with Jolyn Unruh.

"I realized I not only loved theater, I could succeed in it," he said.

Her class and his family's encouragement led him to audition at Walnut Hill, where he continues to compete rigorously for roles. Walnut Hill tries to treat the theater department as the real world, he said, and never guarantees that every student will have a part in each semester's plays.

The school wants to prepare students for the rigors of making a living in the theater. He has practice in competing. In his freshman year, he took part in "Poetry Out Loud" in his English class, with a Jonathan Swift poem. It carried him up to the state competition, where he won second.

"I fell in love with the way poetry felt on the tongue," he said. He has written poetry for as long as he has acted, but writing poetry meant to be spoken has changed his writing style. Speaking each line as he writes it, he listens to the connection and flow and sound of the words, for internal rhyme and repetition. He has become more aware of the relationship between each word, he said.

Kori with family - Senta Reis, Heather and Antoine Alston

"I began writing in the second person," he explained. "When you're sharing something about yourself, it's important that the people listening can experience it as well." Performing and writing lets him connect with himself and with the people around him. "When I write a poem, it needs to be real and raw enough that I would be a little afraid to say it in front of people," he said. And he thinks about what else he can do with his art.

> "Who am I, in essence? I'm an actor, I'm a poet, and I'm a brother."

"I want to create programs for people to be able to share themselves with the world," he said. Spoken word can do that. "What else is this world, but all of our stories? The more I write, the more I understand about people."

He is an older brother, and he has worked with children who don't have one.

"Everyone needs a big brother," he said, "someone to protect them and teach them, and to be brutally honest with them. Who am I, in essence? I'm an actor, I'm a poet, and I'm a brother."

Akwesasne is said to mean, "land where the wild grouse drums." Grouse drum as a courtship display, but in the fall, in the woods near here, a walker at Notchview may hear a grouse launch into flight with a rapid beating of wings.

In the early 1970s, Nancy Bonvillain lived and worked in Akwesasne (or Ahkwesahsne), a Mohawk Territory on the border of upstate New York and Canada. She is now a professor of anthropology and linguistics at Bard College at Simon's Rock in Great Barrington. Nancy has spent time, over many years, learning the language and making friends in a community of the Kanien'kehaka—the Mohawk people do not call themselves "Mohawk." The Mohawk are an Iroquois people, Nancy said, one of the six nations of the Haudenosaunee—along with the Oneida, the Onondaga, the Cayuga, the Seneca and the Tuscarora. Today, they hold land in upstate New York, near Syracuse and Buffalo, Montreal, and Lake Ontario.

"They live in a tiny fraction of their original territory," she said. She came to Akwesasne to work on grammar of the Mohawk language, she said, and to compile a dictionary and a book of conversations for use in schools. As a linguist, she wanted to work in a place where the language still lives, and she lived with families who spoke it among themselves. When she lived there, she could follow a conversation, though her friends there spoke English with her. She returned in the summers and on short visits many times in the next 30 years, she said. At Akwesasne, children now learn the Mohawk language in schools, and the community has emphasized speaking it among families, moving it beyond homework assignments. The 2006 Canadian census reported 600 people speaking Mohawk. The language may still be listed as endangered, she said, but she believes it has a future because so many people are working for it. She recalled a Tuscarora

Nancy Bonvillain

by Kate Abbott

"These communities in some cases are stuggling, like any community, but they have a lot of strength. Look what they've survived."

♥

student at Simon's Rock four or five years ago, Montgomery Hill, who has gone on to study linguistics. Many White Americans, she said, think of American Indians and their cultures as part of the past, as though they have merged into American society or vanished. "We put this into history so we don't have to think about it," she said. "People expect American Indians to live as their ancestors lived hundreds of years ago—and how many American people live as their families lived in 1500? Or expect them to live as mainstream Americans live," she said. She sees them as contemporary artists, scientists and lawyers, musicians and Pulitzer Prize-winning novelists. She sees their sustained efforts to nurture their own languages, schools for younger students, college scholarships, health programs.

In many ways, she said, American Indians today face substantial obstacles in health, longevity, infant mortality and education. Jobs are scarce and promised government funding gets cut from the Indian Health services, education, school lunches and many other programs. Most casinos, she added, do not make large profits—she compared the likely population in Connecticut to a place like central Nebraska.

Though barriers like this are slow to budge, she has seen hopeful signs. In the last 10 or 20 years, she said, she has seen a surge in indigenous rights movements around the world. "The U.N. declaration on the rights of indigenous people is at least a sign of worldwide pressure from these groups," she said.

Near this area, the Iroquois have brought court cases to reclaim land in the U.S. and Canada, to compensate for lost land and to protect and clean up their own land, she said. They may have to live with the effects of contaminated air, land, and water they did not cause. Akwesasne is a Superfund site, she said. (Readers in the Berkshires will understand the challenges of seeking to clean contaminated land and water. The county has similar areas along the Housatonic and Hoosic Rivers.) From helping to teach young Akwesasne students, Nancy has turned to teaching about American Indians in college courses.

Most recently, she has written new editions of textbooks on cultural anthropology and American Indian studies. She acknowledges that anthropology today is a field to enter with care and respect. In the past, anthropologists have at worst made use of other people, she said. Today, an anthropologist might act more honestly, more equally, as a translator—in some ways like a journalist. She feels strongly that anthropologists have an ethical obligation to the people they work with, to advocate for them and to take confidentiality seriously. In any work like this, she would want to be honest and up front, to make sure anyone who speaks with her knows why she is asking questions and what she plans to do with the answers.

As a professor, she now teaches linguistic and cultural studies. Simon's Rock does not have a degreed Native Studies program, she said. Although, its curriculum is both concentrated and flexible; it offers courses, like "Native American Languages" and a cultural studies course on "Native American Religions." In addition, the faculty will willingly coach students in any direction they choose. As they leave for Thanksgiving vacation, she will tell her students to think about all that has happened to bring turkey to their tables. She encourages people who have not yet shared a meal with them to think of the Hadenausee and the Mohicans, the Pequod, the Narragansett, the Nipmuck, the Penobscot, the Pemaquid, the Huron, the Abenaki and all the people with roots in the Northeast, as they are today.

"These communities in some cases are struggling, like any community," she said, "but they have a lot of strength. Look at what they've survived."

In the U.S. and Canada, more than 120,000 people are enrolled in the Iroquois nations, according to the 2010 census. About that many people live in the Berkshires and less than a third as many live in Bennington County. Today, about 12,000 people live in the Akwesasne community, according to the Mohawk Council of Akwesasne, which makes it about the size of North Adams and slightly smaller than Bennington.

Stewart Burns, PhD.

by Margot Welch

Stewart Burns, a historian who grew up in Williamstown, is often asked how a white man, from such a white community, became a passionate, life-long activist and advocate for Civil Rights.

"Even in the beautiful Berkshires, I experienced the ugliness of bullying and ridicule. Facing serious family problems, during my 13th summer I ran away," he says. "But when I got home, I told my parents I would travel around the country next summer. Thinking at least they'd know my whereabouts, they agreed. But that was 1963—the 100th anniversary of the Emancipation Proclamation and the summer that Americans woke up to how real and hateful segregation was."

Burns, a teacher and analyst of social movements, has been dedicated to activism and protest against injustice and the abuse of power. Now Director of Partnerships and Placements at Williams College's Center for Learning in Action, his latest book, "We Will Stand Here Till We Die" (June, 2013), explores the ways the Freedom Movement changed America and shaped Martin Luther King, Jr.

Fifty years ago, the great Voting Rights campaign was born—culminating in the Congressional Voting Rights Act recently dismantled by the United States Supreme Court. In 1963, major protests began desegregating Birmingham's department stores and businesses. Reverend Dr. King was jailed. Young people, who knew the 1955 Montgomery Bus Boycott, left schools to join protesters and encounter attacking dogs, water cannon, and prison. Governor George Wallace blocked black students from enrolling at the University of Alabama.

> *"We who claim the legacy of Martin Luther King, Jr., must cling to the life raft of nonviolence..."*

In August 1963, more than a third of a million people converged on Washington for the great March for Jobs and Freedom, asking for the justice that, 100 years earlier, the Proclamation had promised them. Then, on September 15, white Klansmen bombed Birmingham's Sixteenth Street Baptist church, murdering four little girls.

"That summer, "Burns remembered, "I experienced and witnessed racism in Chicago and Atlanta. I was the same age as those girls. With the church bombing, everything changed for me. I knew I had to do whatever I could to stop such terrible things from happening."

Having spent decades learning and teaching about change and tracking the achievements and mistakes of social movements, Burns advocates continual, thoughtful engagement in our world.

"People often endorse activism either as excessive idealists or as cynics," he observes. "But the important thing is to learn from our mistakes. Understanding our country's democratic struggles helps empower us as informed citizens. We need opportunities to memorialize. Those four little children represent all the young people who put their lives on the line for Civil Rights in the '60s."

Memorials can move us forward. Organizing a nation-wide effort to mobilize commemorative September events in honor of the four girls, Burns invites high schools, colleges, places of worship, all of us to engage in new conversations and reflections about the state of human rights in this country.

"We all need to re-commit ourselves to the aims of racial and economic justice. Always entwined, these are now inseparable from environmental justice and peace." The challenges confronting the country today are new and as momentous as they have ever been.

"The Supreme Court's undoing of the Voting Rights Act in June—well, yes, but I'm one who sees every crisis as an opportunity. Racism, poverty, war, and global warming—these are four interwoven crises facing us. But the young people I've been privileged to teach for the past few decades really understand complexity and connection in ways we never did. When they assume positions of power, I believe they'll find ways to lead with ideals, pragmatism, and compassion."

It is a moment of anniversaries; 150 years since the Emancipation Proclamation and 50 since the March on Washington. As King urged us to replace caution with courage, Burns helps us face how deeply the legacies of slavery and the Civil War are still embedded in our culture, economy, achievements, and way of life.

"We who claim the legacy of Martin Luther King Jr.," writes Burns, "must cling to the life raft of nonviolence, in word and deed, in passion and compassion, as determinedly as he did during the last years of his life. The alternative is unspeakable."

Stewart Burns served as a board member of Multicultural BRIDGE.

Resources
Burns, Stewart, *We Will Stand Here Till We Die* (June 2013)
Burns' Website: tothemountaintop.net
Four Little Girls: HBO documentary available on youtube.com
Slavery By Another Name, Douglas Blackmon: video.pbs.org
Boycott: HBO Home Video, 2001
Tracing Center on Histories and Legacies of Slavery: tracingcenter.org

David Heath

by Roberta Dews

Since 2003, Spanish teacher David Heath has taken a group of his students on a trip to a Spanish-speaking region. His primary goal is to give his students a better understanding of the region's language and culture. But David, wanting each trip to go beyond sightseeing, always adds one more goal to the mix: community service.

And so, when he talks about the trip each year to prospective student travelers, he makes sure to drill those points home.

"It's a language learning trip," he said, explaining what he tells his students at Monument Valley Regional Middle School before they embark on their journey. "We have five or six meetings as to what to expect. Hopefully, when you come out of it, your Spanish will be better, and you'll help others."

Before the groups trip to Cusco, Peru, this past summer, the students organized a clothing collection drive for the Peruvian children. Once in Peru, the students stayed with host families, had classes in the morning at Amauta Spanish School, and then worked with local children in the afternoon. In the beginning, the students had to get used to their new environment.

"When they first get there, there's a lower level of comfort with their surroundings because everything is new," he said. But once that new feeling wore off, the students felt energized and got down to the business at hand. "They had the chance to interact and get to know the locals," he said.

Helping the Peruvian youngsters with their homework, playing games like chess, or simply having some fun drawing chalk on the ground or coloring books, the American students got involved.

"It's all about building bridges and communicating with people."

"We had 17 kids and divided them among three projects. Two of the groups were involved in the afterschool program, and then some of them went to a school for the deaf," he said. "With the afternoon projects, (the kids) had to be self-starters. Most of the kids jumped right in."

David has fostered this mix of learning and volunteerism for many years since he traveled to Spain for a mission trip in the 1980s.

That trip "made it so that I was fluent, (and) it gave me a lot of insight into how other people do things." He has also traveled to Mexico and Spain. "After the mission trip, I decided I would get certified in Spanish," he said.

On his most recent trip, he also gave his students room to relax and explore. They visited Machu Picchu.

"We got up at 3 a.m. to get the bus, and then we got to the train station. It was a really

David with students at Machu Picchu, Peru

scenic train ride," he said. "We did sightseeing and then climbed the mountain Winu Picchu. The native Peruvians have a reverence for the earth, so we made an offering. It was a day to be remembered."

Though the trip was hard work, David saw it make a difference in his students' lives. "We were tired in the end, but it was a good tired," he said. Interacting with children who lived in Peru made an impact on 13-year-old Ana Bloom.

"It has changed my perspective because everything there and here is different," Bloom said. "We take a lot of things for granted (here). In Peru, some kids just wanted food." The trip has since inspired Bloom to continue volunteer work in her community.

"I thought maybe I should do it here," she said. Hearing stories like Bloom's reinforces David's mission.

"It's all about building bridges and communicating with people," he said.

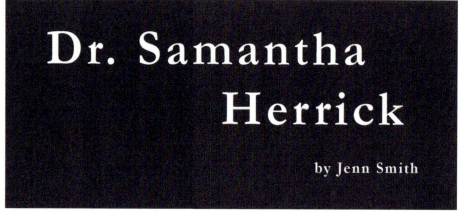

by Jenn Smith

As a Lenox Memorial Middle and High School student, Samantha Herrick '92, was a standout basketball player. In 2013, she was inducted into the Berkshire County Girls Basketball Hall of Fame, as the county's all-time leading scorer with 2,055 points. Today, her basketball days long behind her, Dr. Samantha Herrick is now holding court in a very different arena, researching rehabilitation methods and advocating for people with disabilities. Last summer she bought a home in Lenox, but she still commutes a few times a week to New Jersey where she works as an assistant professor in rehabilitation counseling and community counseling at Rutgers University.

Dr. Herrick has traveled across the country to raise awareness about universal access and recently represented New Jersey and the Berkshires at the United Nations on April 2 for World Autism Awareness Day. This year's theme was employment, and her primary area of interest and expertise is connecting people with a diagnosed autism spectrum disorder to opportunities for higher education and employment. Asked if she knew heading into college that she was heading into this field, Herrick responded frankly, "Oh hell no. And you can quote me on that. Back then, I went to college to major in basketball."

But, as she finds with her students at Rutgers, everyone has a unique pathway for ending up in the field of rehabilitation and working with people with disabilities, including herself. Samantha went to the University of Rhode Island on a full basketball scholarship and half-thought inklings to become a theater major, having been a Berkshire Theatre Festival apprentice and involved with Youth Theater at Lenox Memorial and Shakespeare & Company.

But by the end of her freshman year she found herself struggling with academics, and that summer she was considering not going back to school. An adviser of hers encouraged Samantha to get screened for any learning disabilities. She was diagnosed with Attention Deficit Hyperactivity Disorder (ADHD). Not one to give up, she returned to URI with a new self-awareness and facing new challenges.

"There was a lot of trial and error," she said. She learned to advocate for herself and to get academic accommodations for note taking and doing all of her work through a word processor, she said. She went on to become a communications major, despite her struggles with reading and writing.

"It was all about self-efficacy," she said. "I could demonstrate what I was thinking and always did well in the classroom because I could talk." After graduation, Herrick returned to the Berkshires only to face a new set of challenges, physical this time. "My body had gotten really wrecked from playing basketball," she said.

She had already had surgery on both feet and had hardly played the sport during her senior year. The August after college graduation, she had back surgery. She spent a few years working locally at Berkshire Humane Society and the former Bev's Homemade Ice Cream. One day while working at the ice cream shop, she threw her back out again.

"It was a sign," she said. "Something was telling me to knock it off, and that you have to apply your brains versus your brawn and get a desk job," Herrick said. So she replied to a classified advertisement for a job coach at Berkshire Vocational Services, a program now offered through ServiceNet. Instead, she was hired as an employment specialist, helping people with disabilities find jobs.

> *"[The students] were enigmatic to me, but I also found myself charmed by their incredible range of abilities despite facing other challenges."*

Out of the thousands of people she's worked with since, she still remembers her first client: A middle-aged man with intellectual disabilities who was dissatisfied with being an assembly worker. As someone new to the field, Herrick had to rethink how to communicate with him and to identify what he was capable of and what would make him happy.

"I loved that challenge," she said. "During my first week there, I knew I was home."

By age 25, she was a program manager of vocational programs for Goodwill Industries of the Berkshires, eventually leaving to get her master of science degree in rehabilitation counseling and disability studies at Springfield College.

Her credentials and passion led her to helping students with disabilities at the State University of New York at New Paltz. She not only encountered students like herself, she also began meeting students with a diagnosis known as Asperger's syndrome, now part of the range of conditions classified as an autism spectrum disorder (ASD).

"They were enigmatic to me, but I also found myself charmed by their incredible range of abilities despite facing other challenges," she said.

As she went on to research and present ASD as a doctoral student at Pennsylvania State University, she found that many people, from parents to counselors to doctors, were often at a loss on how to best serve these students, particularly in academic and career settings.

"Even in my own field, there was this unmet need with disability," Samantha said.

That factor continues to drive her to research, educate and advocate for people with disabilities and how to help them pursue high-quality opportunities for advancement.

"I don't go anywhere off-duty," said Samantha, who's constantly tweaking curriculum, pouring over studies, and scheduling speaking engagements.

"My field has a very strong social justice component," she said, noting that people with disabilities are often subject to neglect and being treated in a dehumanized way.

While at SUNY-New Paltz, Herrick once had her students trace how a person in a wheelchair would access a certain school building. They discovered, through a series of corridors, the answers led them to a basement-level door near the back of a loading dock.

She asked her class, "When's the last time we forced people to go through a service entrance?" Asked what society can learn to best effect change for people with disabilities, she said, "That's easy: It's remembering that they're people too."

International Students

by JV Hampton-VanSant

It is not infrequent that I am blown away by the passion, creativity, curiosity and intelligence of Berkshire Counties youth. For five weeks this summer, I had the pleasure of working with English Language Learning (ELL) students from the Pittsfield Public School District. From rising 5th graders to rising high school seniors, each student brought a different perspective, but the high school students also brought a refreshing energy that was unmistakable yet also rare.

These students, the high schoolers especially, were actually excited to learn and excited to be in school. Having moderately recently finished my own education, I can look back on fond memories of the teachers who managed to keep the entire classroom constantly engaged and promoting an atmosphere of learning. Sometimes, through no fault of the teachers, that can be a struggle.

Sometimes this difference in approach is a cultural one. Most, if not all, of my high school students, are immigrants. They informed me that one of the reasons people come to the United States is to get a better education. That because of this, they take education and their futures more seriously than their fellow students. This is not without its risk and it's sacrifices, however. Many immigrant youths have to leave their families.

Estefania Arias, a PHS student, gives us some perspective in a speech she wrote during her class. "If they come here, it is because their families are here, or because they think that their life may be better here. Maybe their family sends them. And this makes me angry because, if their home countries had a better education system, or their own countries were better countries, then the children won't need to come to the USA. When the children are in the USA, they may wish to go back to their countries, but they can't because if they go back, they can't come back to the USA. It is not fair because they may want to go back for vacation or to visit their families. These children, they cannot go back."

Rossana Quispe, a fellow PHS student, said in her speech, "We aren't trying to take your job; we are just trying to have a better future for our families. Immigrants are not what you think. All the myths that they told you are all lies. We are not bad people, as the myth has said. We are loving and caring people. If you get to know us, you'll find the myths are untrue. What you hear can brainwash you."

It is not only Latino students that face these difficulties; being an African immigrant has its own set of challenges. Christina Englyshe, a PHS student, tells us it can be difficult to stay in touch with loved ones.

"Some family members think that, when a person from Africa comes here, they don't have time to call them or chat with them. They think that person doesn't know them anymore.

"We aren't trying to take your job; we are just trying to have a better future for our families."

But Africa and America have different time zones, and some people are busy. People must understand that I haven't forgotten them, and I have not forgotten my family members. People must understand that I still love my family and my friends. People must remember that I still love my family and friends and I will always remember them."

> "We all have dreams, we want to be healthy, we want to be equal. But most of all, we want to be free."

In the US, culturally, we tend to use summer school as a punishment. But some cultures value the opportunity as an opportunity to learn or a chance to actually prepare for the upcoming year. We sought to engage them in many different ways, from teaching them how to play various musical instruments, the importance of banking and finance, to the value of exercise and creative expression. But each time we approached them with a new subject, we were surprised by the knowledge and excitement they had for each subject.

Despite the difficulties each student has to endure in their own personal lives, they still manage to hold out hope for their futures. With the creativity they possess, and the skills they all have, I foresee a bright journey ahead. To quote Ernest Hemingway, "It is good to have an end to journey towards, but it is the journey that matters in the end." And these students have no shortage of goals. As Rossana says in her speech, "We all have dreams, we want to be healthy, we want to be equal. But most of all, we want to be free."

♥

High School ELL student at PPS Gateways Summer Learning Academy

To listen to the student's speeches, please visit:
http://www.youtube.com/MulticulturalBRIDGE.
To read the speeches, visit http://www.berkshireeagleblogs.com/onthebridge

Summer showcase from BRIDGE's Cultural Identity Project, led by BRIDGE instructor, Ann Gallo

Every so often the conflict in Darfur takes center stage in the news cycle. Then the coverage subsides, and many times the interest goes away as well until the latest atrocity captures the spotlight. But even when Darfur isn't a "trending" topic, it is always on the mind of Professor Darius Jonathan, a native of southern Sudan and former advisor to the Vice President of Sudan. Professor Jonathan, who has been in the United States for about 30 years, is a senior lecturer in Arabic at the University of Vermont. He lived through the turmoil of a civil war that has fractured the region for several decades. After receiving an education in northern Sudan and working in the government, Professor Jonathan became more involved in academia, first in Hawaii and then in the northeastern United States.

His experience is something he can never forget, and so he continues to talk about Sudan to keep it on the public's radar. "The ongoing and complicated conflict, which first started over ethnicity and religion between the Africans and the Arabs, also includes rights to autonomy and oil resources between northern and southern Sudan. Thank God (for) some of us who witnessed this," said the Professor, who is proficient in six languages. "This is my perception as a concerned U.S. citizen and as a person from Sudan. It's geopolitics (and) it is sad because I have good friends in the north (of Sudan). There are good people, but it's the fundamentalist government." For Professor Jonathan, Sudan as he knew it, changed on Aug. 18, 1955.

"I was 10 years old. A shooting broke out. Suddenly we saw throngs of people running to us. 'They said, the Arabs are coming. They are killing us.' That was how the civil war began," he said. The division grew between the Arabs and the Africans. "My father (a police officer) was in protective custody because he was suspected of rebellion," he said. The external strife profoundly affected the family. With his dad gone, young Darius's mother, who was pregnant, was left to care for her children, including the youngest son, who was gravely sick and needed urgent medical attention. But it was too late.

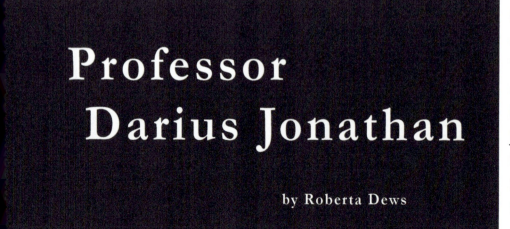

"My youngest brother died, and when my mother gave birth, that child died," he said. He believed that had his father been home, he would have been able to get his brother the care he needed and lessen some of stress weighing on his mother. "My brother would have been in his 50s today. I saw on the face of my parents the agony of losing two kids." His family's pain encouraged him to get an education—making him the first person from his clan, the Marimbas, to go to college, at the University of Khartoum in northern Sudan. The decision to learn and master Arabic was a strategic one. "The best thing to do is to know your enemy better than yourself," he said. However, it's much harder for Professor Jonathan to fathom the staggering loss of life at the end of the war— 2.5 million people. While there were intermittent phases of peace, he said, those resolutions didn't last long once

Professor Darius Jonathan

by Roberta Dews

the government decided to negotiate with rebel groups. "Once that happened, the stipulation was that the government had to do certain things for peace," he said. But instead of peace, the genocide in Darfur began in 2003. The Janjaweed or Arab tribesmen in the northern part of Chad and Sudan, slaughtered men, women and children in Darfur, a total of 300,000 people to date.

"The best thing to do is to know your enemy better than yourself."

"The reason was they were not happy with Darfurians who asked for autonomy," the Professor said. The ongoing genocide, coupled with the bombing of South Sudan by Sudan over oil resources, has left South Sudan ravaged. Despite this tangled web of issues, Professor Jonathan says people can still do something to bring about the eventual change through political pressure. He credits celebrities, like George Clooney, who have used their platform to bring attention to the region. "(Clooney) is doing a wonderful job. What we need to do in this country is to re-educate people about what's going on. Write to your congressman and talk about the bombing of innocent people," he said. "Ask questions. We want congressmen to send a rejection of these politics. The time has come to declare a no-fly zone in some of these areas. Keep the pressure (on)."

♥

Professor Darius Jonathan lives in Williamstown, MA and teaches at the University of Vermont. Originally from the South Sudan, he came to the United States for graduate school at the University of Hawaii. Professor Jonathan lived in Hawaii for fifteen years, and all of his children were born there. His twins are still in college and his older son lives in New Jersey. Professor Jonathan maintains strong connections in South Sudan visiting at least every year. This summer, he visited his family and brought one of his students, in order to begin an initiative focusing on women's health in rural South Sudan. He also collected thousands of books to bring to a divinity school. He plans to continue teaching and working until all of his children have completed school and hopefully retiring around the age of 70.

As she prepared for Christmas with her husband, five children—one son applying to colleges up and down the coast—and a boisterous dog, Mary Makuc looked forward to a week filled with family and activity. Her husband had made dozens of Christmas cookies. Her family is Catholic, she says, and the holiday is a warm gathering and focus for them. With her husband and children and work with local organizations, she is a busy and fulfilled community organizer and an advocate.

At 21, she survived a car accident that injured her head, spine, and leg. These injuries prevented her from walking for a long time, and she still experiences challenges in walking. Her disability crystallized her mission: she works to improve the lives of people with disabilities. Mary grew up in eastern Massachusetts, in a suburb between Worcester and Boston. She was attending college to become a nurse when the car accident injured her.

Her family, her religion, her humor and the fact that she is "an extreme extrovert" helped her through her recovery, she said. When her father entered the hospital room after the accident, he said to her, "Mary, you still have hands," and she responded, "Yeah, and I'm breathing, Dad." She held onto her ability to see positive possibilities and humor in daily situations.

At first, recovery took a great deal of energy, she said. She spent five long months in the hospital before she could move back into her family's house. She then began learning to walk again with the help of medications and physical therapy. Sometimes, she said, she felt as though she spent all her time going to doctors.

Then one night, a friend came over and loaded Mary and her wheelchair into the car and took her to the movies. Her friend helped Mary return to herself by making sure Mary could get out and relax. She continued her studies in social services and graduated with a bachelor's degree. After looking for work around Worcester and Boston, she moved to Amherst. While working there she met her husband, who was living and working in Monterey. Eventually, Mary joined her husband in Monterey, where they still live.

> *It helps when people are honest about their emotions and concerns when they encounter people with disabilities.*

She has worked continuously in social services, in places including Gould Farm, and now while raising her children she pursues projects that will benefit the Southern Berkshires. She is working to form a Monterey Community Center, a local space for classes and other learning opportunities. She serves on the community center's board. She has also applied for a grant to create a dance class in the pool at Berkshire South Community Center, an opportunity for people who have difficulty standing, walking, dancing, or balancing, to learn in the safety and warmth of the water.

She wants to improve the quality of life of people with disabilities, she said, to find ways for them to move comfortably in their communities and for their communities to open to them. Many communities and places have made some effort to accommodate them. Special parking spaces, designated wheelchair ramps and seating on buses give people with disabilities recognition, she said, and she believes they are positive steps, but they are not enough. Recognition happens between people. She said it helps when people are honest about their emotions and concerns when they encounter people with disabilities. It helps when people ask questions, such as how or when someone needs or wants help. Asking is the best thing anyone can do, she said. If they don't ask, people who wish to give her a hand may do the opposite. When she is going through a door and someone automatically assists, saying, "Oh, let me get

Mary Makuc

by Emma Sanger-Johnson

"I would love to see more integration and inclusion."

the door for you," they may not realize she is using the door for help in balancing, and someone taking the door from her might make her fall. She also wants to shape space so people can move through it smoothly. She works for more awareness of the architectural challenges people with disabilities face every day, looking for ways to change them and to help people understand them.

"I would love to see more integration and inclusion," she said. Some spaces are easily accessible for her while others are difficult, and the people who shape them may not know it. "It's straddling two worlds," she said. When she goes out with a group of friends who also have spinal cord injuries, she knows they are going somewhere accessible and the people with her are experiencing the same things she does. But when she goes to local restaurants or stores, she may have trouble getting in the door, and once inside she often has trouble navigating the space. These places are not built to accommodate people with physical disabilities, and she knows this is not intentional, but it is a constant challenge.

She can move around more easily in a wheelchair, she said, and she uses one at home because she can move quickly in it. But the world is not set up to allow wheelchairs everywhere, and away from home she often uses a walker to get around because she can move more freely with one, in more varied spaces.

She sees and pushes against the stigma that surrounds people with physical or mental disabilities, people are too often seen as a burden, she said, as being too slow and awkward to accommodate. People with disabilities have gifts, talents and skills, she said. They contribute to the world, and often they have trouble being recognized outside of their disability.

At the turning of the year, in a time of community and listening, willingness to learn and understanding, she and her friends are here, sharing gifts, reaching out to loved ones, making resolutions, and leading their lives with strength, humor and confidence.

With rolling hills and close-knit community, Berkshire County is known as a place of nurture for artists and musicians, and relationships that last for years.

Bear McHugh, Project Coordinator for Berkshire Area Health Education Center (Berkshire AHEC), grew up in Great Barrington. He is still in regular contact with people he knew as a student at Monument Mountain Regional High School; some of the people he knew then are now employed by the high school. These time-tested friendships have withstood much, including the fact that Bear was known as a completely different person during his high school years.

"This is not an uncommon realization now," he said, "But that doesn't make it easy. Most often, trans people are met with ignorance on the subject."

Bear began to question his gender identity as a student at Ithaca College in upstate New York. He remembers his college years as a difficult time, overshadowed by his Roman Catholic upbringing. He also remembers the love and support of his parents, who sought out the correct information to help him. He thinks the transition would have been smooth if it had happened in high school.

"I really think that, if I were still at Monument when all of this was going down, my friends would have still loved me and accepted me," he said.

Familial understanding, or at least willingness to adapt, can be the most influential factor in the life of

Bear McHugh

by JV Hampton-VanSant

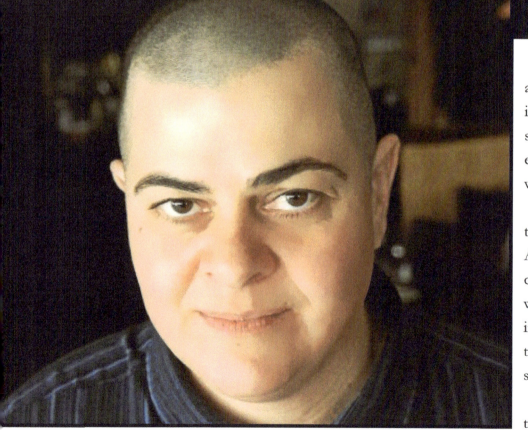

any youth. While a person's gender identity is deeply personal, he said some choose to share their experiences in the hopes that they will benefit others.

Many people facing this transformation have a difficult time. According to national statistics, Bear cited 30 percent of LGBTQ youth will have reported a suicide attempt in the past year. Fifty percent of transgender youth will have attempted suicide before the age of 20.

One of the common contributors to depression and suicide is a feeling

> "Most often, trans people are met with ignorance on the subject."

of being alone and being misunderstood, he explained. Mix loneliness with a lack of information about an important section of identity and those high numbers are understandable.

People who do not encounter outright discrimination often encounter microaggressions. Microaggressions are the little things people say, usually without malice, that alienate groups of people or belittle a group's experience. That alienation is ultimately extremely dangerous to the health and safety of youth. That is why sharing his story is so important: The more he shares the information, the more likely he is to save a life.

"You never know exactly how the information will impact someone," he said.

Now, Bear tells stories and gives information that saves lives by running the Youth Suicide Prevention Project. The project hopes to build resiliency among all youth, not just LGBTQ youth. Resiliency means giving youth the ability to bounce back from depression, bullying and other causes of suicide. For those not at risk, the Project can give insight and the tools to see when someone is showing signs of depression, anxiety and suicide.

Spreading this information can be crucial to developing acceptance. "A little bit of education can go a long way," he said.

He came to this work gradually. After college, he worked as a landlord in Albany for a while. After being sought out for the position, he began working at Berkshire AHEC when the high local suicide rate prompted action. In 2004, Berkshire County had the highest rate of youth suicide in the state. Berkshire AHEC created the Youth Suicide Prevention Project and put Bear in charge. In 2011, Berkshire County had no youth suicides – strong progress.

"I didn't go out looking for the work. It sort of just found me," he said, and he has become passionate about his work.

Bear lives in New Lebanon, New York but spends most of his time in Berkshire County. Living up to the "Class Clown" superlative he earned in high school, he has a smile on his face most days. Despite the heavy topics, he deals with day to day, he rarely gets discouraged. The Berkshires, like the rest of the country, have a long way to go, but he is helping to create a future that looks brighter.

> One of the common contributors to depression and suicide is a feeling of being alone and being misunderstood… Mix loneliness with a lack of information about an important section of identity and those high numbers are understandable.

La Navideña

by Kate Abbott

Mary and Joseph set out from Nazareth to walk to Bethlehem. For nine days, they traveled, looking for a place to stay. Mary is pregnant, in her ninth month, and tired, and they walk slowly in the early nights, looking for some place not too full to give them a floor to sleep on. And here, at last, a door opens. Here is a place to stay. Here is a house with light spilling out onto the winter grass. There is a dinner on the stove, and children singing Noche de Paz, Noche de Amor to a guitar and maracas playing "Silent Night."

For nine days before Christmas, throughout Latin America, families are celebrating La Novena Navideña. Different countries call the celebration by various names—it is Las Posadas in Mexico, meaning "places to stay." It is a saint celebration of the birth of Jesus. Alexandra Belalcazar and husband, Luis Fernandez, spoke for and as part of their community in the Berkshires. "Among Latinos, the cultural base is Catholicism," she said. In South and Central American countries, Colombia, Guatemala, Honduras, Mexico, people celebrate the nine-day journey of Joseph and Mary. Nine days before Christmas, they begin praying, calling for Jesus to come, and they sing traditional Christmas songs and carols.

She and Luis want to pass on this tradition to their children. Here Christmas is celebrated differently, they said, and they wanted their children to know how they had celebrated as children in Colombia.

Maria Quizhpi of Great Barrington, who came to the Berkshires from Ecuador, first celebrated La Noveña Navideña here. Her children and their cousins acted out the New Testament Christmas story, dressed as Mary and Joseph and the shepherds and the wise men.

The Reverend John Salatino, the pastor at St. Mark Parish in Pittsfield, saw the celebration at Maria's house and encouraged the community to continue the tradition, and under his authority the event has expanded.

Now, families will go from house to house, to a different house each evening. On warm December nights in Colombian towns and cities, families gather with their neighbors, everyone on the block. Here

> *"For nine days before Christmas, throughout Latin America, families are celebrating La Noveña Navideña."*

"The children radiate peace and happiness."

the houses stand farther apart, and snow makes driving more difficult. But when dozens of people come to a small house in the mountains, almost on the Connecticut state line, to sing, the warmth is tangible.

In Colombia, the celebration begins nine days before Christmas and ends on Christmas Eve. On Monday at midnight, people will stand outside, waiting for the beginning of Jesus' birthday, and they will play music and stay up through the night, keeping vigil.

Here, this year, La Novena Navidadeña will reach its final night on Saturday; it begins early so that the families can be together on Christmas day. The community will gather in Sheffield at the American Legion Hall, and all are welcome to join them. "God is for all," Luis said. The celebration is in its seventh year, he said and growing. "Children are always at the center," Alexandra said. "God says children are like aromatic perfume for their innocence. They have pure, clean hearts." They may run around and make noise, she said, but they are welcome and praised. Young girls perform in a Christmas pageant. It is not a competition, Alexandra explained.

Each has a banner as the princess of love, of peace, of friendship, of community. And all the children perform with music and dancing they have practiced for more than a month. The girls wear white dresses, and their caballeros, the boys who dance with them, wear suits.

"The children radiate peace and happiness," she said, "doing this dance they have practiced, and maybe not doing it perfectly, but it seems perfect when everyone is laughing." They memorize their parts to re-enact the Bible story of Jesus' birth. Here is the angel coming to Mary, and Mary pondering these things in her heart. Here are Los Reyes Magos, the three kings, saying we offer you and holding out their gifts.

"The Shepherds offer their songs," Alexandra said, "because they are poor."

♥

After 28 years in Housatonic, Massachusetts, The Reverend Mr. Edward Shaw and his wife of 37 years moved to Pittsfield, Massachusetts, and into the very first house they have ever owned. For 31 years, he worked for the Rising Paper Mill, which became the Fox River Paper Company. When the local owner sold the Housatonic mill to a rival company, Neenah Paper, in 2007, Neenah closed the mill within two weeks. According to public records, 137 people lost their jobs.

"It was a tough time for me," he said, "thinking I had spent 31 years in a secure establishment that I could retire and care for my family." He grew up in a family of nine children, his mother had been raised Catholic, singing "Adeste Fideles" with her twin sister every year at the Christmas Eve Mass in Lenox Dale.

"We had tough times, but we learned through those times we struggled financially," he said. When his father became ill and could not work, the family came together. "You did yard work, you raked leaves, you shoveled snow, and you gave the money to your mom because that might be your dinner that night," he said. Sometimes, he would come home to find the lights out until they could pay the power bill. In that time, neighbors helped neighbors and his family supported one another. "We dealt with it," he said.

The Reverend Edward Shaw

by Kate Abbott

He started working at Fox River when it was still the Rising Paper Mill. Rising was a private, family-owned company, he said, and, in 1976, Robert O'Connor sold the mill to another private company, owned by Robert Buchanan. Rising and Fox River were a lot alike, he said. Small orders kept them afloat in tough times. Because they were a smaller company, they could take on smaller orders that larger companies ignored. They made many kinds of paper and were known for art paper. Their source of water was an artesian well, he said. Their customers valued their paper so highly that when Neenah announced that the mill was closing, one of their largest customers tried to buy the mill, he said, to keep it running. He did shift work and moved to different jobs wherever the company needed him. He worked the paper machine and in the beater room where they prepared paper to be machined. But he spent most of his time in the finishing department, converting paper: taking the paper made on the rolls and running it through cutters and guillotine trimmers, getting it wrapped and sealed into boxes and sent to the shipping department. He spoke well of O'Connor as a boss.

"He knew your family, he knew who you were. He'd

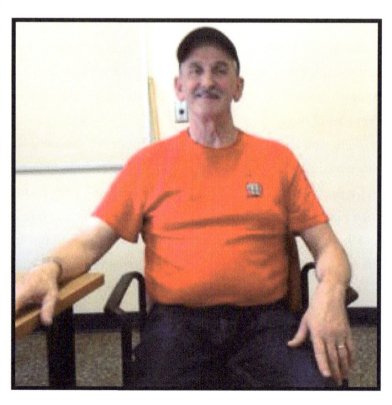

come down on the floor [to say] 'How're things going? How's your wife, your children?' He came down at holidays. People got free turkeys. We've gotten away from what makes us go."

Edward became Vice President of the union, representing the workers and negotiating contracts. It takes skill, he said, to sit at a negotiating table. "You have the company on one side and the people on the other, and you're pulled from both sides," he said. "You try to represent people as best you can for their own good, and you have to look at the company's side also. They're trying to make a business work. We represent the business, and we want to be compensated for our hard work. And sometimes personalities can get in the way." When the negotiators had reached a compromise, he would then have to present it to the people he worked with, and they could reject it by a vote.

"You have to go back and explain," he said.

Rising Paper Mill, Housatonic, MA

"People felt the union was so powerful, if we didn't get what we wanted, we could just strike and get it that way. It's not true. No one wins in a strike, and the biggest loss is to the workers." He saw only one short strike on his watch.

"You hammer out the hard issues and make a go of it," he said. And they did until Neenah stepped in. When Neenah first bought Fox River, he said, staff members were glad to be bought by a large company with public stocks. They never anticipated they would be shut down. The closing was a time of heartache for him. Young people just starting their lives had new cars, new homes, and babies and now had no jobs. "BerkshireWorks got involved with them," He said. "I'm sure a lot of young employees went back to school. Times are tough. We know that now. A lot of manufacturing jobs have gone overseas."

"When something like that happens, you feel devastation. You feel bitter, why did this happen to me? But you do what you have to do." He worked at Monument Mountain Regional High School for a year in 2007, then came to his present job as an evening custodian supervisor at Muddy Brook Elementary School. "I feel blessed to have this job," he said. In 2007, too, he was ordained.

He now serves as a Catholic deacon for St. Peter in Great Barrington and Blessed Teresa of Calcutta in Housatonic, both parishes under the care of the Reverend William P. Murphy. Reverend Shaw became Catholic at 21, returning to his mother's faith. Later, he took courses for his ordination at Elms College for four and a half years while he was working 10-hour days at the paper mill. He remembered the day he first heard a Catholic Mass, by chance after a folk concert, and the day, after a year of study, that he first knew he wanted to become Catholic. He had gone up into the mountains in Vermont, where his brother and his in-laws had a camp. He sat on the hillside above the reservoir to watch the sun rise. And that morning he felt a warmth, he said—his spirit became alive.

Upon meeting Nyanna Slaughter, the first thing you are likely to notice is her height. Standing at 5'10 in sweat socks, she has a statuesque form and flawless face more akin to a model then a star athlete, but then you'll notice the gym bag packed and ready for a quick departure and the green and gold team suit that is a main staple of her wardrobe.

She was born and raised in Berkshire County and started in sports at the early age of four when she learned to play soccer and basketball at the Pittsfield YMCA. From that tender age until today, sports have been a constant in her life. As a senior at Taconic High School, she

> "I can't wait to go to college. I'm looking forward to getting a more complete view of the world."

is also the captain of the basketball and volleyball teams, she plays for a travel team, attends church nearly every Sunday with her parents and she has even co-starred in a short play called "Enuf!" which was based on the true-life stories of Nyanna and eleven other young Pittsfield women.

"[Enuf!] started out as simple writing exercises within my Rites of Passage group," she said as she thought back a year ago. The Rites of Passage and Empowerment Program for Girls was founded in 2009 and is a program that emphasizes the holistic (mind, body and spirit) self-discovery of its participants. Enuf! Was inspired by an OBIE Award-winning play by Ntozake Shange, and was developed by playwright Yvette "Jamuna" Sirker and Spoken Word Artist Nakeida Bethel-Smith.

The Slaughter Family

Offered as a personal and poignant look at the experiences of young women of color living in the Berkshires, the play debuted to a packed crowd and its popularity sparked a demand for more show dates throughout Berkshire County.

"The next thing I knew, we were collaborating and helping to develop a real play and then we were on stage performing it. There was a scene about hair that was mostly improvised by [us girls]. It was a lot of fun just coming up with that." Aside from her brief, yet successful stint as an actress, Ms. Slaughter has a long list of accolades and awards as proof of her hard work and commitment including a recent sportsmanship award bestowed upon her by referees and coaches throughout Berkshire County. Although she has proven excellence in athletics, her academic standing is impressive also.

"I've made the high honors list every year since middle school. I've only missed one day of school since the third grade and last year I received the Outstanding Algebra 2 Award." She said, naming a few. She has also received several Dean Merit Scholarships from various colleges and universities including New Haven University, Curry College, A.I.C. and Western New England University. To say that Nyanna's athletic and academic records are impressive is an understatement but sports aren't the only passion in this 17-year-olds life.

"I plan on attending the Henry C. Lee Institute of Forensic Science at the University of New Haven in the fall where I'll be studying criminal justice for crime scene investigation. Dr. Lee was on the O.J. Simpson case and other high profile cases. When I'm in his class, I'll have the opportunity to visit actual crime scenes. I'm very excited for that and I'm just [as] excited about working in that field. I can't wait to go to college. I'm looking forward to getting a more complete view of the world."

Many of us have been enthralled by the countless criminal investigations shows on television at one time or another and it was those types of shows that sparked her passion for crime scene investigation.

You would think that a dedicated athlete such as herself would be glued to every primetime pro-game in the lineup, but that's not the case for Nyanna.

"I originally started watching *"Criminal Minds"* but then I got hooked on *"C.S.I."* Just this past Christmas my family wanted to watch the game, but there was a C.S.I. Marathon on. I watched it for four hours before my Dad made me change the channel," She said with a smile. Before she could rush off to yet another practice session, she was broached with this question, "Where do you see yourself in ten years?"

Nyanna Slaughter

by Nik Davies

"In ten years, I'll be living in a beautiful home, possibly in Atlanta, Georgia with my dog. She's an Alaskan Malamute. I'll be working in crime scene investigation and people will call me Sargent Slaughter!" she said with a giggle.

Her first trip from Ghana to Ohio must have been extraordinary for Kuukua Dzigbordi Yomekpe, working today as Residence Director at Bard College-Simon's Rock. Raised in a suburb of Accra, lush, green, warm year round, with yards full of fruit trees, she had never been to America, known such cold, or seen snow.

"Big trees were bowed down with ice," Kuukua said. "And Columbus was so different in so many ways—organized, with street names and so many white people! At home, churches are everywhere, right next to houses, and worship is active. Everyone singing, dancing, hugging, shouting and praying together."

Kuukua Dzigbordi Yomekpe

by Margot Welch

As a self-described "perpetual student," Kuukua realizes her commitment to pursuing education. "By the time I was eighteen, I understood that education was what gave people access to money, power, and control. At Ohio Dominican College, I took Human Resource courses. But I'd always loved writing and ended up majoring in English."

Kuukua grew up an ardent, literal believer in the Roman Catholic faith. After college, she enrolled in a Master's program in Theology at the University of Dayton. During her first year there she worked in Student Affairs as a graduate assistant in campus ministry. But her journey took a new turn.

"I believed some texts were sacred, written by God, and not to be questioned. And I was a Bible Quiz champion—even went to national competitions! We were looking at faith through many lenses. There were gospels I'd never known about, which had been excluded from the Bible. It was unbalancing. I decided to leave graduate school."

Lucky for us, a professor convinced Kuukua to change her itinerary. She completed her English Master's degree with an emphasis on postcolonial and adolescent literature, even studying in Morocco for a semester. And, as Assistant to the English department chair, attended an international writer's conference in Egypt where meeting and hearing the powerful voices of African women writers was inspiring.

"Though I did not yet feel I was a writer," she said, "I started believing I could be part of something important, something bigger than myself." Student Affairs took her next to work as the First Black Rector at the University of Notre Dame. It was gratifying to deliver a range of essential support, advocacy, and counseling services for all the students. She started new programs that included providing health information to sexually active young people. She organized an African dance group and offered Bible study group for gay and lesbian students who were quietly struggling to align belief in the Bible with their 21st century identities. She'd found her calling: to help young people discover themselves safely while they learn about the world and move towards adulthood.

From the University of Notre Dame, she journeyed west to the Graduate Theological Union, in Berkley, CA. It was there that she completed her Master's Degree in Psychology. She also achieved certificates in Women's and LGBT Studies, before beginning another Master's program for an MFA in Writing at the California Institute for Integral Studies. Her thesis is a memoir, entitled "The Coal Pot: One African Woman's Journey to Self-Discovery."

Kuukua and Students

When a Student Affairs opportunity at Simon's Rock came along, she traveled east. Here, in addition to counseling and advocacy, she's taught African dance and cooking and started a writing group for girls who, like Kuukua, are finding their own authentic, integrative voices. But, she notes, for students of color, Great Barrington is conspicuously white. "Light-skinned or bi-racial people seem more easily accepted around here, but there aren't many of us dark ones. People usually stare and it can feel lonely: we wave when we see each other. In Ghana, I never thought about being black – only about the reality of being a woman in a world where men have power and control. A special feature of my calling is for students of color to know that people who look like them and me can accomplish, succeed, and overcome any obstacle."

> "I believed some texts were sacred, written by God, and not to be questioned."

Now securely identifying herself as a writer–memoirist, essayist, and writer of social commentary, Kuukua's blog "Musings of an African Woman" (ewurabaempe.wordpress.com), is courageous. And, on this leg of her great journey, she's working in a "secular setting," enjoying the challenge of developing non-religious ways to support students' spiritual growth. "In many ways this job is what I dreamed of doing when I began studying Theology because it means working in a communal setting. Like a village where, together, we are all helping to raise children as responsible adults who find ways to do what they themselves are called to do."

Kuukua Yomekpe is beginning her second year in the Berkshires, continuing as a Residence Director at Bard College at Simon's Rock. At 37, she has decided to stay here a little bit longer before making her next move at age 40. She dreams to start a catering company, maybe a restaurant in order to pursue her love of cooking and food. During the summer of 2014, she was published in two journals: "Pentimento" and "Fierce Hunger: Writing from the Intersection of Trauma and Desire" She continues to write and update her blog.

"They are, in effect, still trapped in a history which they do not understand; and until they understand it, they cannot be released from it...And if the word integration means anything, this is what it means: that we, with love, shall force our brothers to see themselves as they are, to cease fleeing from reality and begin to change it."

~James Baldwin

Children of Multicultural BRIDGE

Eiko Brown

by JV Hampton-VanSant

It's midway through a bright Monday. The sun is giving us a preview of the summer to come, and a slow, gentle breeze floats refreshingly. On a day like this, it is easy to see why someone would return to build a home and raise a family in Dalton, warmed by the feel of a safe and close-knit community.

Red-Karpet Tattoo on Depot Street holds the pleasant aroma of candles. The walls are decorated with portraits inside ornate bronze and antique gold frames. Burgundy velvet rope barriers section off the tattooing area. The same burgundy velvet, outlined by intricate bronze back frame, covers an antique settee where Eiko Brown sits during the interview.

Brian and Eiko Brown moved to Dalton in 2012. Brian is a native of Dalton, but Eiko comes from a small town in Japan called Tsu, in the Mie prefecture, close to Kyoto and Osaka. Eiko's family was open-minded, she said and appreciated the benefits of travel and adventure. Eiko's father was a member of a group who did volunteer work in countries worldwide. Eiko was drawn to the openness, the freedom and the artistry in the U.S.

"I loved the language and the music and knew that was where I wanted to go," she reflected.

At 15, she came to America for the first time as an exchange student in Chicago. She immersed herself fully in learning English. When she came as an exchange student, she remembers filling out the form and checking off not wanting to be in a large city where she would run the risk of falling into a specific community.

"I chose a place with very few Asian people," she said. "I wanted to make it possible for me to learn the language and practice only English. I find it's the best way to learn a language: to be completely immersed in the culture."

When she returned to Japan to finish high school, she felt differences between the U.S. and Japan. "In Japan they teach you to work in groups, and there is less of a focus on individual performance. If you fell behind, there was an entire group to support you," she said.

Eiko has always been artistic, but when she came to college for business management, she began more and more to practice drawing the world around her. There she met her husband, Brian, who inspired and encouraged her to practice the photorealistic style she'd been using and to consider portraiture. When she and Brian moved to Dalton, they opened their tattoo parlor. He is the tattoo artist. She draws portraits at the shop.

She spends hours focusing on all of the miniature details, down to each hair on the customer's head. She said a lot of the work she does with portraits is memorial, so accuracy is the highest priority for her. She also designs tattoos. Eiko's own tattoos are exquisitely detailed. While her family is open-minded and expressive, Eiko said there was not much acceptance of tattoos in Japan.

"There are still places out there where you cannot use a public pool if you are tattooed," she said. In traditional "old-school" Japan tattoos were very large and some were associated with the Yakuza (originally peddlers, traders, and gamblers, now criminal organizations). But that has changed. Now more people have tattoos, she said, and they hold deep meanings and in many ways reflect the person who wears them. A lot of detail and precision goes into custom tattoo work, she said.

"In Japan, each tattoo covers the full body and tells a folk story," Brian said. "The tattoos are not selected by the client beforehand but determined by the artist after long conversations." Symbols carry intricate meanings in Japanese language and writing, Eiko explained. The pictogram for one word may hold a story.

Eiko and Brian Brown

"In Japanese, when we write the Kanji for the word 'person,' we know it is a simplified version of a much

> *"In Japan, each tattoo covers the full body and tells a folk story."*

more traditional piece of art," she said. "The traditional symbol for a person resembles a man standing, being held up by another man, and the reasoning behind that is, you can't have just one person. We, as people, hold each other up. So every time we write this word, this is what it means."

Though Brian was raised in Dalton, both he and Eiko experienced culture shock returning to the Berkshires after time in such a diverse place as San Francisco. Eiko said the Asian community in the Berkshires often feels comparatively disparate and small. It is strange not to have easy access to certain shops she might see in Chinatown in a larger city, such as Asian clothing stores, hair shops or Ramen bars. The numbers are growing, but the group tends to stay in its individual subgroups (Japanese, Korean, Vietnamese, etc.), and she sees less unity here among them than she found in San Francisco.

Reflecting on her experience, Eiko said, "When I first arrived, I was pretty sure people knew me mostly as 'Brian's Asian Wife', but as time went on, people got to know me through Red-Karpet and through my art. The Dalton community is very supportive, but I would love to see more diversity."

In the future, Brian and Eiko hope to start a family, and they hope to raise their kids in an environment that embraces many languages and cultures. They look forward to spending more time in the Berkshires, celebrating the various cultures that exist around them.

Portrait by Eiko Brown

Thirteen years ago, Winnie Chen and John Yeung opened The East, an Asian restaurant in Great Barrington that prides itself on serving the best of Chinese and Japanese cuisine.

"It was hard in the beginning," Winnie recalls. "Imagine starting a restaurant in a town of 10,000 people with more than 50 restaurants already! But my husband's family had always had restaurants. We take tradition seriously. Continuity and community are important to us." Not easily discouraged, Winnie has long been one who looks ahead. At least since she was twelve, in the 1990's, when her parents brought her and her brother from Guangzhou, a large Chinese city in the southern province of Canton, to New York City.

Winnie Chen
by Margot Welch

"I don't remember ever missing China. We were all together, and my grandparents and great-grandparents had been in New York for many years. In some ways, it felt a little like coming home. I'm a fourth-generation American citizen, my grandfather even served in the military."

Winnie's husband, John, grew up in Great Barrington, graduated from Monument High School and Berkshire Community College, and knew he would follow his father into the restaurant business. But after high school in New York, Winnie, whose father is a contractor, became a full-time student at Hunter College, working two jobs and determined to find the right career path. After trying Nursing and Psychology, she settled on Accounting, a great asset for the restaurant, where she often spends twelve-hour days.

"My days can be long but I enjoy everything I do. Most important is our family. My boys are at the age when we can teach them our values—not just by telling them, but by what we do. In taking good care of them, they understand how much family matters to us. I remember watching my grandparents age and seeing, from how my

> "My days can be long but I enjoy everything I do. Most important is our family. My boys are at the age when we can teach them our values..."

Mom cared for them, how important it is to respect our elders. One day we'll be the older ones. My sons know that. It's all about recycling!"

Winnie is optimistic, cheerful, and wholeheartedly devoted to her family and her work. She visits her parents and grandparents in New York frequently and is determined that her children will learn about Chinese traditions and culture. Each summer the boys spend two months with their New York grandparents, attending an intensive all-day summer school program to study academic subjects and Chinese. As a professional businesswoman, Winnie brings young Chinese men and women interested in learning the restaurant business to be trained at The East.

"And I can help them find ESL classes, even teach them beginning English myself if they want. We're always looking for people who want to learn. Continuing education is very important to us too. A few years ago John spent six months working in a five-star restaurant in Hong Kong himself, in order to learn new culinary skills and recipes." When Winnie and John bought their restaurant, it was a used car dealership.

"All that's left of that property is the glass in the front windows," she says, smiling. Every few years they redecorate the East: today it is a happy combination of bold, optimistic reds – the traditional Chinese color for good fortune, and handsome, dark wood latticework. Their extensive menu changes only a little from time to time, but they always offer a special menu for people who want to discover traditional Chinese dishes cooked in new ways. "Many people tell us they come to us because they know we'll always have their favorite dishes. And now, in addition to our specialties, we also offer Japanese cuisine. Our hope is that The East will be predictable, well loved, and up-to-date."

Focusing on what's worked well in the past and what might make the future even better, Winnie feels very fortunate, grateful for her family, her work, and her community.

"In my family, nobody talked about the past. I never think about it. But I feel very lucky. While tradition and Chinese culture are very important to us, so are the hopes that my parents and theirs had in coming to America. This is a big, free, fair, see-a-future country where we can find a good education and better life for the next generation."

♥

Alfred Enchill believes family is the fabric of life, but he also knows the family and community are interwoven. The Ghana native was 25 years old, married and in business hauling bulk mail for the Postal Service when he immigrated to Bridgeport, Connecticut in 1988.

Eventually, he made his way to the Berkshires, where he and his wife opened their own business, Elegant Stitches, in Pittsfield and settled down to raise their four sons.

"My wife designs clothes, and she used to make garments from traditional African cloth and then take them to trade shows and fairs," said Alfred of how the pair came to start Elegant Stitches. "There was a company in NYC that was buying some of her clothes, but one day when we made a surprise visit we found they were just taking the designs and mass producing them."

Out of frustration, the Enchills decided to go into business for themselves and started manufacturing clothes and doing custom embroidery in the basement of their home.

"The embroidery sold well, and we realized there wasn't another embroidery business in town, so we started one. Three years later we moved it from our basement to the corner of First and Fenn streets into a retail store, and we bought more equipment. Business was going well until February 7, 2004.

"That's when the story gets better," laughs Alfred. "Someone torched the building. An arsonist." They lost just about everything. "But it was also when we saw the people of Pittsfield show real generosity and affection," he said, recalling the outpouring of support from the community in the wake of the devastation.

> "Someone torched the building, an arsonist... we saw the people of Pittsfield show real generosity and affection."

"People offered trucks…the fire department, the police department, even our bank. My banker was the first person to call to tell me 'if there's anything you need.' And the kids' principal sent food. It was really something, our phone was ringing off the hook. We got notes from people we didn't even know."

He was even offered space on Tyler Street to relocate, and given three months' rent free as he was getting back on his feet.

"We stayed there six years before we bought this place," he said. But Alfred didn't wait six years before he started giving back. In 2005, a year after the fire, he and other community members founded the United Africans of the Berkshires, a non-profit organization dedicated to helping newer immigrants assimilate more easily.

"Things went much smoother for me than the average person who immigrates," said Alfred, noting that when he arrived in the late 80s, he had an uncle who had been in the country already for a decade. "When I first moved [to the Berkshires] there were only four African families. Now there's so many I don't know them all. When people come in, many times they come in blind. They know they need documents and inoculations, but there

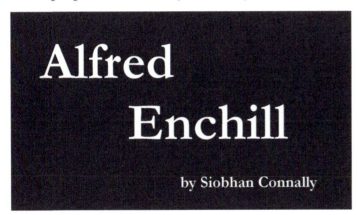

Alfred Enchill

by Siobhan Connally

can be real culture clashes and all of that comes into play." Cultural and religious differences can seem trivial in the abstract, but often in practice they can be upsetting. Even something as simple as illness can cause some consternation.

"From time to time someone will get sick, or have a baby, and every time an African is admitted to the hospital everyone goes in to see the

people. Everyone, not just immediate family. It's how we do. Family is the community. And that saying you've no doubt heard 'It takes a village to raise a child?' That's something Africans find most difficult to do in America.

"In Ghana you can leave your child at home and not worry. You could leave them and know the neighbors would be there. You can't do that here even when they are teenagers, it's too scary." And while that is one aspect of Ghana that Alfred misses, he also realizes that his non-African neighbors miss those bygone days as well.

"The culture draws you into that element. We all struggle to find time and one income can't do it. I tell people all the time: Don't cut corners with your kids. To get the right results, you have to be there. The timeframe you have with them is so short. The fabric of the family gets pulled apart, but it's gradual. When you realize it, it's often too late."

Many years after the war John Fülöp distinctly remembers the train ride he took from Amberg to Bremen and seeing nothing but piles of rubble. John was eight years old. To this day he will never forget the scope of destruction he saw through the windows of the train taking him and his family from Hungary to the German coast and finally, the USS Holbrook and America.

In October 1944, John, his parents and his maternal grandmother were living in Budapest and the city's bridges were being blown up, one by one. Knowing the city would soon be isolated and that an enemy attack was imminent, they were waiting for a truck to collect their furniture so they could leave to stay with relatives in the countryside. It didn't arrive and, hearing an enormous explosion, they left for the train station—wearing only the clothes on their backs. Just outside Budapest, the train stopped and sat, far into the night.

"(After) my mother went out to look, saw (enemy) troops, (and) heard them singing, we all got out, beginning our long walk through the war—by foot, train, and truck convoys, always heading west, toward Germany, where we thought the Americans would eventually be…to get away…"

From the many difficult months that followed, John does not remember every detail. But, some images remain vivid—corpses, dead horses, town officials hanging in public squares, ruined houses, running through fire to safety. When gunners boarded trains they were riding, the Fülöps rushed out, ran ahead to the engine, and crawled under the train to hide. Thousands of refugees were walking west as they were, on highways where there were enemy attacks.

John Fülöp

by Margot Welch

"Once a fighter plane started strafing [us], everybody ran into the ditches. When my mother saw (the plane) coming back for another run, she pulled a woman's dead body over us so we wouldn't get shot. A little pull of the trigger was what life and death were all about," John said. One night, he recalls, they were welcomed at an Austrian youth hostel, told they'd be safe and crawled into their first real beds in weeks. But during the night enemy soldiers arrived and lit up flares before dropping bombs.

79

"These bombs were big," he remembers. "If one didn't kill you, its impact could. The building next door collapsed, crushing people. Everyone ran to the shelter, screaming. There was no air; it was dark….my family made a circle around me. My mother asked me if I was scared. 'As long as you're with me, I'm not afraid,' I said."

After many hard months the Fülöps settled in Plattling, Austria, sharing a one-room home that was probably a former POW camp, he suggests. Every day he walked an hour each way to school; his father found work in the kitchen at a nearby American military camp. With remnants of fabric and yarn, his grandmother and mother made clothes.

By 1950, the Fülöp family lived in an apartment in Flushing, New York. The new and different culture to deal with was difficult for everyone, he said. His mother, an accomplished pianist, started giving lessons. His father, though trained as a lawyer and working as a Hungarian government statistician, never adapted so easily. He took a job at a plastics factory—to learn English, they thought—but he never left. Only after he'd retired did his son learn that, working there, his father had realized a private dream to one day be a mechanical or industrial engineer and design machinery.

John lived at home through grammar, high school, college and beginning graduate school. With a Master of Architecture degree in 1967 from Yale University, he worked for years in New York City as a architect, photographer, multimedia artist, and slide film producer. Having spent weekends in the Berkshires for years, in the late eighties he moved with his family to West Stockbridge. He has always been determined to nurture and strengthen his communities, and energy efficiency has been consistently central to his design and construction of beautiful, sustainable, and affordable buildings.

Now, for example, he brings his expertise and commitment to the Community Land Trust Board. As a child, surviving life on a continent broken by war, he couldn't have predicted the global warming that is central to his concern now about our world. He's now writing a paper linking Zero-Energy Building to "Smart Growth," focusing on alleviating the devastating consequences of climate change, urging us to see ourselves as caretakers of our planet. He knows firsthand what can happen when worlds are lost.

"I always have to find something to do that I think is important," John says. "Maybe it was riding through Germany, seeing all that, and thinking, 'I need to do some building.'"

> *"These bombs were big. If one didn't kill you, its impact could."*

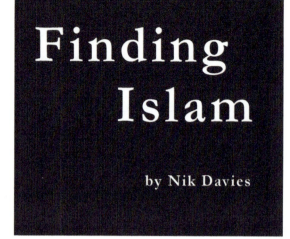

Finding Islam

by Nik Davies

In the United States today, there is a growing populace of female Americans that have embraced Islam. Many of these women are married to Muslim men and often face the misconception that their conversion to Islam was forced upon them by overbearing husbands instead of their own understanding and acceptance of the faith. Such is the case of Anna, an American-born woman from a devout Catholic family and her husband Raffi, a Muslim bred in the Islamic faith. They live in Western Massachusetts but have asked to be quoted under pseudonyms to protect their friends and family.

On a snowy December night, at a holiday party in Boston, Anna was introduced to Raffi. Their meeting seemed like divine providence or perhaps a dose of destiny. Their time together was magical until about a month into their blossoming relationship when Anna learned that Raffi was a devoted Muslim who practiced Islam.

"Initially, I was scared. Raised in a Catholic home, I didn't know what to think." Like Anna, some Americans would be shaken by such a revelation. Islam is purportedly one of the most misunderstood religions in the West, and for many, the Islamic faith is still inherently linked with terrorism and anti-American sentiment from the Middle East. But being rational, spiritual, educated and in love, she endeavored to understand the truth in being a Muslim.

"I learned. I read books and watched videos. I wanted to understand what Islam really meant. I discovered so much and found that many Muslim people truly understand their faith and it impressed me." Through education and patience, she soon developed a respect and deeper understanding of Raffi and his faith. So when he asked for her hand in marriage, she accepted. But breaking the news to her parents nearly brought their relationship to an end. "When I first told them, they were very upset. They made me watch the movie, 'Not Without My Daughter' and it terrified me." A true to life story released in 1991, the film depicts the escape of an American citizen and her daughter from her tyrannical husband in Iran.

Muslim women in the inner-city

"I understood [why they did that]. They were affected by the media and television." Raffi stated. "They didn't know me and the things they heard about Muslims and [saw] Muslims do, were quite bad. They love their daughter and they were afraid for her." Despite her parent's uneasiness, Raffi and Anna were soon married. My parents are devout Catholic people and raised me the same. I never thought I would change and Raffi never asked me to change. But the more I learned about Islam, the more it resonated with me. There were so many similarities between [Catholicism and Islam] that it wasn't that much of a transition for me."

To name a few similarities, both religions require mandatory fasting such as Lent for Catholics and Ramadan for

Muslims. Mary is held in high esteem in both The Qur'an and The Bible and both religions believe that the worship of their God should be continual and daily. In 1985, Pope John Paul II corroborated this idea when he declared to an audience of thousands, "Christians and Muslims, we have many things in common as believers and as human beings. We believe in the same God, the one, and only God, the living God..."

"I was very sick once," Anna remembered. "I had a cyst the size of a football that had to be removed. Raffi told me to say, 'Hemdu Lellah'. I thought that might work for you, but I don't think it will for me." Anna said.

"It means 'Thank God' in Arabic," Raffi interjected. "She was sick and in pain. She couldn't see what there was to be thankful for? But perhaps God put her in that situation to avoid something worse. It's like if you get a flat tire today and are late for work, don't get upset. The flat tire was put there to possibly prevent you from a more serious accident down the road. Perhaps that flat tire saved your life." Raffi said.

"It is a different way of thinking, it's freeing," Anna said. "Since I've embraced Islam I feel as though things in my life have been tweaked and perfected. I love my [parents] but sadly this still causes strain on our relationship. Sometimes it's really good, then something will happen in the news and it will be hard again. But they try and they even send us flowers on our anniversary."

Hassan II Mosque, Casablanca, Morocco

> "...educate yourself...search beyond the images some media outlets might represent."

"I'm not worried about it," Raffi said with a wave of his hand. "I will continue to give them time and patience. We will not give up. In time, they will know who I really am and they will truly love me."

What of Raffi's family in his home country of Morocco? "His family loved me immediately. They are amazing people and there is never any judgment. They are my family and I love [visiting] them." Anna said.

When asked what she would say to someone who may not understand the Islamic religion or her decision to embrace it, she had this to say, "I don't have all the answers but I would say, educate yourself. Try to understand and get past any stigmas you may have and search beyond the images that some media outlets might represent."

After sixteen years of marriage, Raffi and Anna are still going strong. "Islam teaches that all things are a part of God's plan. We believe we were meant to meet each other, we were meant to fall in love and we were meant to be married. This is our happily ever after and it will be forever improving."

Have you or your child ever played soccer in Berkshire County? Have you experienced the occasional trip to the hospital or perhaps taken a Spanish class in school sometime in the past four decades? If so, then you probably know Luis or Grace Guerrero. Luis, a soccer coach and Spanish teacher, and his wife Grace, a lifelong nurse who retired from Fairview Hospital, have a long history of caregiving and community service here in Berkshire County. But their journey first began in Quito, Ecuador, where Luis answered an ad in his local newspaper.

Posted by the U.S. Consulate in 1961, the ad offered a teaching position at a private boarding school in Monterey, Massachusetts. After a grueling application process, and despite being the youngest and least experienced out of the

154 applicants, Luis was awarded the position. He soon left the warmth and comfort of his birth country and found himself alone in the frigid air of Southern Berkshire County.

"I didn't know anyone [in the United States]," he said. "From my family, I was the first to leave my country. I was excited and eager." For four years, he lived at the Avalon School in Monterey, working 24-hour days, 6 days per week. He was teacher, tutor, athletics coach, and often father and mentor to the students there. He fit in well in his new position, but the transition was challenging in a way that Berkshire natives may not realize. "I was afraid I would forget my language," Luis said, as he relived his first few years as an American citizen. "There was no one to speak Spanish with. I loved going to St. Peter's Church in Great Barrington because, at the time, they spoke Latin and it was as close to Spanish as I could get."

To remedy his lack of conversational Spanish, Luis offered Spanish lessons to local elementary school students. The idea caught on with a rush. "I started teaching Spanish to one second-grade class in the grammar school and the children, parents and teachers loved it so much they wanted all of the grades to be taught Spanish. So, I taught Spanish. Soon I was traveling from one school to another to another. It was wonderful." After years of hard work at the Avalon School and a growing demand for Spanish lessons in his community, he was ready for a much-needed vacation.

"My goal was to travel from [Berkshire County] to Ecuador by car. I was single, aggressive and a little bit crazy to do that."

"My goal was to travel from here to Ecuador by car. I was single, aggressive and a little bit crazy to do that," Luis said as he described his 22-day journey from Berkshire County to Quito, Ecuador. But because of this incredible trip, Luis reconnected with his longtime friend and pen pal, Grace, and after years of friendship, they decided to marry. Grace came to the U.S. in 1966 and almost immediately began work at Fairview Hospital.

"I was getting a physical at the doctors and during our conversation he discovered that I was a nurse. He told me they needed nurses at Fairview hospital so he set up a meeting for me. I went to the doctor on Friday and by Tuesday I had a job as a graduate nurse. The difficult thing was I didn't know the language very well. Soon I was raising children, taking care of my home, working and trying to pass the nursing board exams with very little English but I was always learning. The patients helped me with English; the nurses helped me with English, the people were absolutely fantastic. We love it here and Luis has worked very hard for our community," she added. "He has done a great deal with our young people. Before Luis, there were no Spanish classes in Berkshire County."

He was indeed the catalyst in instituting Spanish language education in many Berkshire County schools and, at 75, he is still an active substitute Spanish teacher. He is also an honored and lively soccer referee and an avid community volunteer. "But teaching Spanish is my passion! Sometimes, we even have soccer games entirely in Spanish. The children love it." he said with a smile.

When asked if he misses his home country of Ecuador, Luis had this to say, "The first 10 years of my life in the U.S., I spent longing for Ecuador. I love Ecuador but now I go to the post office, the bank, the library and supermarket and I know most of the people. I've been a soccer referee for years. I doubt there is a kid in Berkshire County that doesn't know me. Berkshire County is my home. My wife, brother, children, and grandchildren are here. The people here are our friends and they have all become our family. I speak their language and they speak mine."

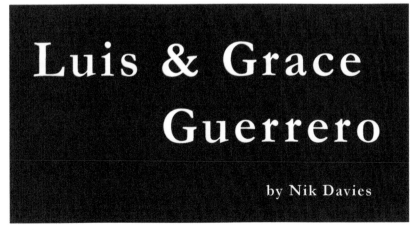

Luis & Grace Guerrero

by Nik Davies

The Mahida Family

by Margot Welch

Life would be different for the Mahida family if they were still in India. With hired helpers caring for their house and children, Jignesh Mahida, an electronics engineer, would probably be working for a large company and his wife, Rita, free to pursue a career. But, like most immigrants, the Mahida's came to America for good education, opportunities, and better futures for their children.

Jignesh Mahida became owner of Mountain View Motel in Great Barrington on Christmas Eve 2009 where he and his family, including his parents, live. His father had a long career as a successful mechanical engineer in Gujarat, where engineering has contributed significantly to the region's commerce and trade since ancient days. Until 2009, when the youngest Mahida child began school, Jignesh's mother had never worked outside the home.

Were he living in Gujarat, Jignesh's days would start early as they do here. Waking and showering, he'd walk to the temple for Morning Prayer, come back for a light breakfast, and leave for work at eight. Home midday for a

Street life ~ Ahmedabad, Northern State of Gujarat, India

lunch hour with Rita, he'd finish work at six pm, and come home for tea, prayer, and dinner. Everybody in the family would eat together.

"Here our days also begin with prayer and tea," he explains. "We take short calming walks. But in India, men go out and do the hard work. Women have defined roles. Though things are changing, some fine Gujarati ladies with professional credentials still choose to stay home because we believe a mother needs to be with her kids, teach them, and keep the home. Here Rita and I share housekeeping, cleaning all the rooms together every morning. After lunch, prepared by Rita, I go to a Certified Nursing Assistant training program. Rita is home to welcome the children back from school, give them snacks, help them bathe and change. But at 4:30 she leaves for her part-time job at Subway. We have a plan for each day, and we must all help to save money so our children can go to college. We live here, we accept the situation, and it's a good life!"

In 1996, Rita's family left Gujarat to join relatives in Pennsylvania, when parts and packaging departments in big companies were hiring so many Indians there was no need to learn English. In 1998, Rita's family began looking for a husband for their daughter. Through networks of relatives and friends they found Jignesh, who was then completing a three-year engineering degree. The two married in May 1998.

Do the Mahida's foresee arranging marriages for their children? "Certainly if they want us to," Jignesh answered. "We'll talk about it with them. But we know it may be another story. They're growing up in a different world. As a peaceful person, I will not argue. I'm doing my best to teach them all the lessons that have been important to us. But the final decision will be theirs. I never want our family peace compromised because of fighting." Uncles and cousins on both sides own motels in America. Why do Indians find this business so appealing?

"That's easy," Jignesh answers. "In the family, we trust and help each other and share resources. With motels, we achieve two things—a home for our whole family, and a way to make a living. Here in Great Barrington, it's a safe, quiet, peaceful neighborhood where my guests tell me they have never slept so well. This is important to me. It's in the Indian nature to be helpful. And, with my family here, we can maintain our cultural and religious traditions. We've already taken the children home once for a traditional ceremony. But we see the differences. Though kids here are on their own when they turn 18, we continue to depend on our parents and nurture our children. Family is always a presence in our lives." First-generation immigrants commonly share homes. Slowly, generations move apart – around the corner, into different neighborhoods and, eventually, farther away. But sometimes we all long for relatives nearby. Family, even when it's absent, is a universal 'presence.' At the Mountain View, guests are welcomed like relatives by members of a helpful, kind, hard-working family that are glad to see you with them, here, in a new world.

Jignesh Mahida was born in Gujarat State in India. After receiving his engineering degree at Maharashtra University, he completed further computer certifications there before moving to the United States to join his wife in 2001. He lived in Pennsylvania until 2009, when he and his parents gained US citizenship. The family decided to open a business and chose the Berkshires to make their new home. Jignesh recently completed his CNA certification and he will begin working at Fairview Commons Fall 2014. For the future, he may go back to school and become a medical interpreter. There are many options for the future, he says, but his priority is to provide education for his children.

Dr. Homer "Skip" Meade
by Siobhan Connally

By any rational measure, Dr. Homer "Skip" Meade has led a charmed life. An intellectual life. A life that has always examined truth and decency. For more than 40 years, the W.E.B. DuBois Scholar and Cornell University graduate has made his home in Western Massachusetts. He has taught in local and regional schools, served as a member of the W.E.B Du Bois Department of Afro-American Studies at the University of Massachusetts at Amherst, and has been involved in crafting curriculum and teacher standards to ensure future academic excellence for a new generation of Americans.

So it is hard to imagine him, now wearing the uniform of professorial distinction, ever brandishing a rifle and wearing the garb of revolution. Risking his own life to gain a valid education for others. That is his truth, as well. Dr. Meade is among 24 distinguished local African-American men who spoke at Pittsfield High School in celebration of Black History Month. He and his father, a professor and Boy Scout executive, began to train African American youth in the skills they needed to obtain advancement. His mother was the Director of Youth Services at the Morristown Neighborhood House, where she grew an organization that provided child care, daycare and after-school programming for families, many of them immigrants in transition. It's an organization that continues to this day.

"I benefitted from all of that," says Dr. Meade. "They wanted those examples to be understood and inculcated by me that there was a purpose and that certain individuals within the culture had certain things they had to recognize and live up to. He had been class president, he had gotten an appointment to West Point but ended up attending Cornell University.

"What I found at Cornell was an absence of inclusion of individuals of color in activities, which had excluded them," he explained. "A most striking example of this was DuBois. But within science, within literature, within those expressions, even architecture, there needed to be a reference to a broader inclusion and process and that's what all the upset at Cornell was about."

His life could have easily ended one day in April of 1969 when racial tensions at Cornell came to a head, and a group of African-American students took over Willard Straight Hall in advance of a parents' weekend. Straight Hall, a student union building, also served as a hotel for visiting parents and dignitaries on the Ithaca campus and would be teaming with people. It started out as a peaceful protest, not unlike other sit-ins that had taken place around the country. However, when members of a fraternity tried and failed to forcibly evict the demonstrators, some occupiers left and returned with guns for protection—Skip among them. He returned to Straight Hall with a 30:30 rifle. "If they didn't meet demands, we weren't going, it was up to them to get us out," he said, noting that the climate of fear at the time played a pivotal role in student resolve.

Just prior to the takeover of Willard Straight Hall, a cross burning on the grounds of a women's dormitory spurred the need for immediacy. "Nothing we saw (in the response from Cornell officials) addressed that. The university couldn't provide better security so we said *We'll protect ourselves*."

Meade knew the potential consequences. He knew what could happen if the school turned to State Troopers or the National Guard to handle the situation. "South Carolina State University, a black institution, in '65-'66 they had demonstrated because the bowling alleys were segregated. And when they got back to the dorms, police, either state or local police arrived and began firing in dorm windows. Several students were killed. That was a real demonstration that the lives of certain individuals had no reason to be respected. It was clear. I knew I had to do something. It's a moment, yes, but there were many, many things that led up to that."

He had prepared himself for the worst. Looking up at a photograph made of him after the takeover had ended—an iconic image that had appeared in Newsweek and which showed Dr. Meade and other protestors carrying guns and wearing ammunition belts as they left Straight Hall, he describes the moment and the appearance of his younger self wrapped in a shroud and carrying a rifle at the ready.

"I don't take this picture lightly," he explained. "I wanted my parents to understand that I had prepared for what was coming. I went up to a room, there were guest rooms in the Straight, and showered and cleaned from all the exertion and sweat that I'd been involved in that day in securing the building. I'd thrown away most of the garb and took a bedspread and folded it and cut here and here, laced with sheet, so dad would know when he came that I'd prepared myself."

That moment caught on film and all the decisions that had led to it were life changing, not only for Meade, but also for countless students who have followed him. Dr. Meade credits the University Provost for his courage in not only brokering a peaceful end to uprising but also realizing the truth of the situation: That while the university had moved to diversify its campus it hadn't adequately prepared systems that would support that diversity and nurture its success.

"We were very lucky to have a Provost (Dale Corson) who understood all that. Truly understood it. It's amazing to think back about it now, back in '66, '67, '68, how attuned he was facing a monolithic structure, he was able to start programs bringing in minority scholars to the university programs to alleviate that which had been long ignored. Saying 'ignored' is maybe stating too much intention. It was just part of the process.

"These professors who believed they were in an ivory tower. Here were students who had been brought into this new recruitment program and put into an economics course and told what the urban economic problem was and here were these students who came from that urban landscape saying that's bullshit."

Corson persuaded the President to allow him to handle the uprising within the University, and not to call outside authorities. The result was a peaceful end of the situation and a change of policy that allowed the creation of the Africana Studies and Research Center, which is still vital today. Dr. Meade still marvels at the outcome and what could have been a very different ending to his story. But he knows such truth, like physics, isn't relative.

"If there is an injustice, we have to right it. When there is justice, then we need to promulgate it. It's not enough to do. To understand the impact of the impact so we can be true and contributive citizens. There needs to be movement of knowledge. That's what I've done."

> *"If there is an injustice, we have to right it."*

A continuous flow of traffic sweeps through State Road in Great Barrington, a busy corridor lined with restaurants, specialty stores, and boutiques. The hectic pace is usual for this active stretch of road clotted with travelers from all parts of the county and Connecticut, too. But inside the unassuming storefront at 67 State Road No. 2, better known as Maria's European's Delights, the tempo is markedly slower. Without the hustle and bustle, patrons are free to peruse the aisles, stocked mainly with Central and Eastern European products with a spattering of Turkish items, and to have conversations with the owners, and sometimes with each other.

"It's like coming in and talking to a friend," said Kris Sekowski, who opened the business with his wife Maria nearly five years ago, "It becomes like a family. Old customers call us by name; we're more like a friendly, neighborhood store." Most of the shoppers who come through have an accent, so when they speak Kris said he can tell right away where they hail from.

"I know who's from where, because everyone is talking. I recognize people by accents. I know already who is of which country," said Kris, who immigrated to the U.S. in 1979 at 24 and still retains a robust Polish accent. "Anybody that walks in always has a story to tell." This kind of environment is a throwback to the local mom-and-pop stores of years ago. And also reminiscent of the ones Kris and Maria enjoyed in the Greenpoint section of Brooklyn, New York, a longstanding Eastern European enclave.

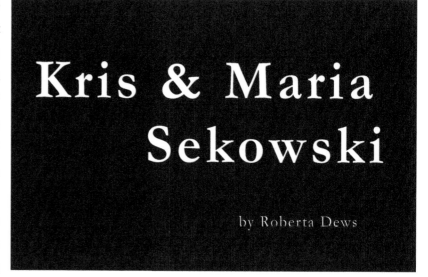

Kris & Maria Sekowski

by Roberta Dews

"[Ours] is the only store of its kind in Berkshire County," said Kris, "but we used to live in Brooklyn and there's a store like this on every corner." The city's Polish specialty shops drew many people, like Maria's parents, who had a weekend home in Housatonic, back home to Brooklyn, New York, to purchase familiar foods. The trips were more frequent leading up to cherished holidays like Easter and Christmas for items like uszka [Polish mushroom dumplings] or stuffed mushrooms," Maria said. "When we came in 87, Housatonic had a lot of Polish," she remembered. "All these people have passed on. There were these Polish picnics. Women used to meet and make pirogues, stuffed cabbage and get ready for the picnics."

"My parents had bought a house over here and we used to come every weekend. Back then, we used to go to Brooklyn to do our shopping." While it would have seemed natural for the Berkshires to have a similar specialty market back then, Maria said she couldn't recall anyone venturing out to open this kind of store. "Years ago, people didn't take (those) risks. Now people just do it," she said.

Though the Polish community that Maria once knew isn't as large as it once was, the store serves as a link to keep everyone connected. "Not so many people know there are so many ethnicities," Kris said. "We are a center point." With customers boasting a spectrum of Eastern European roots, Kris said they focus on stocking their shelves with highly desired staples like vinegar-based foods, marinades, cabbage, mushrooms, potatoes, cheese, meats, and jams. They keep the prices low by picking up the products themselves. Here you can get a good-sized bottle of natural mineral water for $1.

"You have to know your product: That's number one," Kris said. The couple works with several distributors to ensure

Kris Sekowski, Sophia D. Lee and Maria Sekowski

a steady variety. The array of foods resonates with customers, he said, thinking of one particular German lady who always comes in with a list. One young customer was happy to see a European brand of milk chocolate in the display above the front counter. "I was surprised when a kid came in and was so excited to see Kinder. In Europe, they're very popular and pretty tasty," he said. Over time, the products have developed their own calling card, allowing Kris and Maria to forgo ongoing advertising. "We advertised in the beginning," said Kris, adding that they still do some advertising for certain special occasions. "Some people pass by and may come in, but a lot of our customers are by word-of-mouth. That's how people find out about us." And when they do step inside, Kris will offer brief explanations, for those who would like it, on the product offerings, as most are not in English.

But there are also those times when customers know exactly what they want. An actress who starred in *Mamma Mia!*, and shall remain nameless, came in towards the store's closing. She found what she wanted and left, said Kris, who recognized her but kept it at that. "I respect the privacy of my clients," he said. "They just want to come to a small store and not be bothered."

> *"Old customers call us by name; we're more like a friendly, neighborhood store."*

♥

In Loving Memory of Kris Sekowski

Maria Sekowski was born in Poland and immigrated to the United States in 1965. She lived in Brooklyn, NY where she met her husband, Kris. They moved to the Berkshires in 1987 to get away from the city and raise their four children. Together they opened Maria's European Delights, originally on State St. in Great Barrington. In January 2012, they moved the store to Pittsfield. Kris died in July 2014, and Maria plans to continue with the shop but she is still adjusting to this loss. Everything is up in the air, she says, and she is taking life day by day.

For centuries, immigrants have been seeking a home in the Berkshires. Though the landscape of immigration has changed considerably over the last century, the Berkshires continue to welcome people from many parts of the world. The Italian family of Sonsini look back to an earlier wave of European immigrants.

Joe and Theresa (née Troiano) Sonsini own Main Street Cafe in Stockbridge and 528 Cafe in Great Barrington. Joe's parents came with an earlier generation of Italian immigrants to settle in Stockbridge. Three of his grandparents immigrated from Italy, and one grandparent came from the Ukraine. Theresa's parents were also the first generation, descending from Italian immigrants, who arrived in New York City around 1928. Joe and Theresa met on a job in the early 1990s, and they have been married for 19 years. They show pictures of their children around the Main Street Cafe. They had four children but lost the second one to cancer about 10 years ago. The photographs show the family active and relaxing. Joe said he loves being outside and makes it a point to bring the outdoors into their family routines.

Food has also always been a part of his history, he said. His maternal grandmother worked as a cook in a restaurant, and she worked her way up to own her own restaurant. In Joe's family, meals were served at specific times and everyone gathered to eat together. Today, his nuclear family gathers at Theresa's parents' home every Sunday after church.

Being Italian comes with being Catholic in Joe's family and in Theresa's, he said. In his childhood, the family's communal life outside of home and work was organized around their local parish. His parents taught catechism, and he laid bricks for some of the many construction projects around the church. He laughed as he said the stereotype of Italians loving to eat, being loud and passionate and sometimes prone to outbursts, is partly based on truth.

"They are a passionate people," he said. They eat well, work hard and play hard. Being passionate sometimes means disagreements, he said, but generally they deal with them at the moment and move on, with no hard feelings. Sonsini and his wife have always been hard workers, an ethic he credits to their fathers. "They worked almost round the clock to put food on the table and yet rarely missed a football game or

Joe & Theresa Sonsini

by Kuukua Dzigbordi Yomekpe

recital," he said. He and his wife together have about 50 years of the cooking and restaurant business under their belts. Their penchant for good food and community led them to purchase Alice's Restaurant. Two years later they took over the Main Street Cafe and Market. Almost 20 years later, they purchased the old Friendly's in Great Barrington and renamed it the 528 Cafe.

"Theresa is the mastermind behind everything," Joe said. He blends construction and management of the properties, and he plans to renovate the Stockbridge facility in the next year. "It needs a make-over. It's not been renovated since it opened about 17 years ago," he said.

The Berkshires and its diversity play a significant role in the cafe menus, he said. The Sonsini try to incorporate foods from around the region and from different ethnic groups in their planning: gyros, chicken marsala, and shrimp carbonara. They also try to follow the seasons. Butternut bisque soup, New England clam chowder, pumpkin French toast with syrup, walnuts and cranberries, or a French toast sandwich dripping with cheese and a choice of bacon, ham or sausage. They make "American fare" like hamburgers and ribs with locally grown produce and meats from Berkshire and Columbia counties. The Sonsini treat many customers as family, often greeting people by name as they stroll in asking about their lives.

"The usual?"

"How is Jaime?"

"How was Joey's game last night?"

These questions roll off the tongues of the baristas and wait staff as they busy themselves fixing the "usuals" as well as putting in orders with specifications for vegetarian, gluten-free or "no nuts, please."

Joe welcomes guests as his father did. He remembers his father as open in his outlook in approaching diverse people and incorporating ideas and values from different cultures, he said. He does the same today, following in his father's footsteps. Thinking about immigration and assimilation, Joe said he laments not having had the chance to learn Italian. Early waves of immigrants shed their native language and culture intentionally to fit in and become "American." This is different from the approach some have to assimilation now, when preserving language is key.

"*All are welcome here... come give us a try.*"

The Sonsini are keeping the Italian traditions of good food, gregariousness, and welcoming, open arms as a daily part of their work and their lives. Both cafes have cheerful staff, and the Sonsini mingle and chat with customers even when the cafe is bustling.

"All are welcome here," Joe said. "Come give us a try."

Chief Michael Wynn

by Emma Sanger-Johnson

Chief Michael Wynn of Pittsfield is a man of color, and his skin color masks his Polish heritage, as his career masks childhood difficulties. His career as a police trainer and chief of police is greatly influenced by his experiences as a biracial man. These less-discussed aspects of identity, especially his Polish heritage, are important to him and integral in his current success. Born in Pittsfield, he also lived in Southern Berkshire County in Otis and Lee before returning to his birthplace for high school.

"My family, my brother and I, in particular, had a typical American upbringing," he said, "Thanksgiving, Christmas and Easter—every holiday—but with a Polish twist." He was raised primarily by his mother and his mother's family, and he spent time with his grandparents, uncles, and aunts. His great-grandparents separately emigrated from Poland and met once they were in the United States. The essence of being Polish, for him, is tradition and family. He cherishes cultural artifacts like food, clothing, and language which remind him of his childhood and his heritage.

Chief Wynn believes the best way of understanding and learning about someone's heritage and cultural background is to ask about food. "If I described the Thanksgiving meal at my grandmother's house, you could easily see my heritage," he said. "The table setting included pierogi, kielbasa, kapusta, gołąbki." Despite eating typically Polish foods, most people cannot identify this part of his heritage. He continues, "Most people can figure that out [that I'm Polish] from hearing those foods. They might be shocked looking at me that there wasn't other stuff [collard greens] on the table."

In addition to being biracial, he experienced the difficulties of growing up in a single-parent, lower-middle class household. Despite these possibly negative circumstances, positive opportunities including his love of learning and mentors led him to pursue higher education. After spending three semesters at the Naval Academy, he transferred to Williams College, where he graduated with his Bachelor's Degree in 1993. Then he did "what any other recent college graduate would do" and returned to Pittsfield. He knew he wanted to pursue federal law enforcement as a federal agent, and he needed law enforcement experience.

"There was an opportunity to go to work for the City of Pittsfield," he said, "working for the Police Department, not in the Police Department on one of their first community outreach centers. One of my first assignments was recruiting people to take the police exam. I thought it would make sense to know what I was talking about, so I took it. I was then selected to go to the Police Academy."

Chief Wynn decided to stay in local law enforcement. With guidance from his commanders and supervisors, he became a certified police trainer and then began to work in the Police Academy. He became a sergeant and became a fellow with the Drug Enforcement Administration with their Leadership Development Program. Following rapid departmental shifts, he became Chief of Police.

As part of his current work, Chief Wynn trains police officers in cultural diversity and bias crimes, a job that calls upon his own background. As someone who has been misjudged, misunderstood and

> "When you share your commonalities with people, it makes it easier to make progress."

misrepresented, he is able to empathize with other people from diverse backgrounds. Chief Wynn is misjudged and misunderstood as an African American man whose culture is primarily Polish; he is not immediately viewed or identified as a Polish man. People focus mainly on his skin color and assume his identity based on it. By leading trainings and partnering with Multicultural BRIDGE, he is placed in situations where he is able to discuss his experiences being misjudged.

During a follow-up meeting for Multicultural BRIDGE's dialogues on race, he encountered a mother who was angry about her son experiencing horrific treatment in the school district, presumably for reasons related to his race. She felt she wasn't being understood and heard and she assumed that Chief Wynn could not understand her experiences. However, Chief Wynn assured her that he did indeed understand, because he has experience being African-American and of mixed heritage in Berkshire County.

"When you share your commonalities with people, it makes it easier to make progress." He considers this hidden part of his identity indicative of the American experience. "It is uniquely American that you can have these cross-cultural experiences that are hidden," he said. Diving beneath skin color, names, and clothing reveals less-examined facets of peoples' culture and heritage, he said. Physical attributes are still important, but there is a larger story to learn and understand.

The table setting he described, including typically Polish foods, is only accessible through joining him for a meal at his grandmother's house. Stereotypes sometimes supersede true identities. As a Pittsfield native, he recognizes different neighborhoods. Southeast Pittsfield has houses made of concrete, concrete fences and concrete grottos, markers of the Italian stone masons who historically lived in that area. Fences and lawn ornaments are different in other parts of the city because of the ethnic groups who once occupied those neighborhoods. Physical markers express the history of Pittsfield and the progression of the city throughout the years, but the character and identity of the city come from more than architecture. Dated stereotypes, such as areas off of Wahconah Street being typically Irish neighborhoods and Seymour Street being the Polish community are not necessarily relevant in modern Pittsfield. Industry has changed in the city, altering the population. The past does not have to shape the future, he stressed.

When asked to speak at the Women of Color Giving Circle Graduation Ceremony he worried about how to approach the audience.

"I'm seen as a political figurehead," he said, "and instead of talking about what greatness we expect from them and whatnot, I talked about my own history." He called upon his history as a biracial child raised solely by his working mother. In spite of these circumstances, he pursued an illustrious career. The central message was clear—seize every opportunity and do not worry about the difficulties in front of you.

"If I could do it, a kid of mixed heritage from a single-parent household," he said, "then anyone can."

Chief Michael Wynn was born and raised in Berkshire County. After attending Williams College, he began working in the Pittsfield Police Department. He had a very busy summer due to the influx of gang violence in Pittsfield. The continued community conversations surrounding solutions to youth violence provide a source of hope for the future. He plans to continue his work and build a new police station.

Young Voices Matter

by JV Hampton-VanSant

In the ongoing turbulence following the killing of unarmed black men and boys, and the failure of grand juries to indict the police who shot them, three young Berkshire County African-Americans involved with Railroad Street Youth Project spoke about these events.

Kiana Estime, 18, said that her first feelings on hearing that Policeman Darren Wilson would not be indicted for the killing of the unarmed Michael Brown were disbelief, fear, passion, and responsibility.

"My responsibility is to continue the passion to protest, to not stand by and allow this to happen," she said. "I have a responsibility to let friends know and to allow them to be aware of the systemic racism in this country."

She referred mostly to white friends, but also to friends of color, because she believes that her generation has had a need to deny that their color makes a difference. Getting rid of that denial may make them vulnerable and insecure, she said, but it is necessary to address the issue head on. She also thinks there is a fear among her peers of bringing up controversial issues to do with racism. Particularly in what are called microaggressions, things said to people of color that are perhaps not intended to be racist, but, in fact, are because they stem from unquestioned ideas white people have grown up with. These people may mean well, but they cause hurt and anger.

The first step, she said, is to get at the root of systemic racism: the misrepresentations, misunderstandings and social injustices that still prevail for people of color today. "If you don't solve the root, there is no desire to change," she said.

Protesters standing in unity

Tymell, 24, who asked that his full name not be used, said he didn't watch television news about the non-indictment of Michael Brown's or Eric Garner's killers.

"Watching makes me too angry," he said. Commenting on the public outrage towards the justice system and the riots after the verdict, Tymell compared the media coverage and the social outrage over the killing of people of color to emotions experienced after running over a squirrel. "You feel bad for a minute, but then you're over it," he said. He sees this public outrage as fleeting in this society, a society in which the murders of these young black men are dismissed as though they do not matter. "That's what we are to these people: roadkill. All because of the color of our skin," he said.

These kinds of murders are not new and have been ongoing for quite some time, he said. For him, the recent tragedies are personal. When he was 12 years old, he said, living in Brooklyn with a foster family, he had an older brother who was called J Happy, and Tymell looked up to him. J Happy was on the verge of going to college. One day he took Tymell to the park, as he usually did.

"The next moment," said Tymell, "a white cop pulled over and accused J Happy of having drugs in his pocket." The encounter ended with J Happy being shot in the head by the policeman. There was an inquiry during which Tymell was interviewed, but there were no repercussions for the policeman except for his gun being taken away.

"I went through hell there," Tymell said. The policeman was a local beat cop, and Tymell had to see him on a daily basis until he was moved to another foster home.

Originally from Uganda, 21-year-old David, who also asked that his last name not be used, has lived in the United States for almost 12 years. "I've had my share of run-ins" with police, he said, citing an instance where he and a white friend pulled a prank on Halloween. David was suspected and questioned, he said, not the friend. David has watched the news about Ferguson and Staten Island and the many protests with his brother.

Example of microaggression from Buzzfeed

"It feels personal to a degree," he said. "The legal system is not what it should be." He pointed to the fact that district attorneys have to work closely with police and, therefore, have a conflict of interest in how they handle a police shooting. "How do you get the bias out?" he said. "How do you fix a system that doesn't know it's broken?"

> "How do you get the bias out? How do you fix a system that doesn't know it's broken?"

Where is the hope for young African-Americans in all of this? Tymell does not believe there is much hope. He thinks it will take a much larger tragedy before white people wake up to the reality and engage in the conversation.

"I want to hope," he said, "but I don't believe it's going to happen without some kind of purge that will grow out of the frustration and anger being felt by the country." David looks to a new governmental system to create change and give hope.

"How do we make action make something that works? There needs to be checks and balances.," he said in how police shootings of unarmed people are handled and in the justice system as a whole. "Hope is in the struggle," he said.

♥

JV Hampton-VanSant is the Youth Engagement Coordinator with Multicultural BRIDGE. He worked closelsy with Cynthia Pease, an active NAACP member and volunteer from Real Talk On Race with Multicultural BRIDGE, to help youth successfully navigate and record this conversation as the Black Lives Matter movement took root following the murders of Michael Brown and Eric Garner in 2014.

Mike Zabian cuts a striking figure as he strolls in front of the Main Street building that bears his name. Wearing dark gray slacks and an orange, wool sweater-vest, the retired haberdasher seems fit and youthful as he surveys the sidewalk, smiling at passersby.

"I fell in love with this building," says Mike of the stately 19th century structure at 15-19 Main Street, which was constructed, inside and out, using Lee's famous marble. For years, as he commuted past the store to his various jobs, he dreamed of one day owning the place. Back then, Mike was also a customer of the men's shop that inhabited the ground floor.

"You can't build this anymore. Having this place was like a dream. You know?" It's been over fifty years since Mike Zabian left his home in the village of Mdoukha, Lebanon for a new life in America. With little more than a single $20 bill and an education, Mike found himself in Western Massachusetts, married, and on his way to creating a family business that has become part of the fabric of the Berkshires community. He was just 16 years old.

The Zabian Family

by Siobhan Connally

"My wife was already in America. She brought me over," he laughs. "I was 16 when I got married. I needed to have my father sign for me because I wasn't of legal age." Mike's wife, Mary, came from the same village in Lebanon but had come to America in the early 1960s. The two met when she returned to Mdoukha for a vacation from her work in Springfield. For years, the couple worked long hours at menial jobs. Neither were discouraged by setbacks. Hardship only made them work harder.

"I applied for a job at the Smith & Wesson factory in Springfield when I was 18. They told me they'd call in a couple of weeks, and when they called they said they had no job for me. I just went to the factory and told them someone had called me for a job. They told me to go get the physical and I got the job." Together Mike and Mary have six children, and over the years have nurtured almost as many businesses.

"Our first business was a package store and nursery in East Lee," said Mike, who bought that business in the late '60s and expanded to include flowers, which was a hobby. By the late 70s he'd managed to buy the building on Main Street and the clothing store, by the mid-70s, he'd opened a fine jewelry shop. For a time, all of the businesses ran simultaneously. He worked around the clock.

"When you have six kids you work day and night," laughs Mike, who went on to say that hard work and honesty are the most important aspects of success. "Everything else is just common sense. You have to learn from your mistakes, and I thank God for them. There is no human being that doesn't make mistakes."

His son, Mohamed, who now owns Zabian's Fine Jewelry, said that for him, there was no question about going into the family business, even though his parents wanted him to be a doctor or a lawyer.

"I was born into it. I was 8 years old, helping to run the register. It's not like working for a paycheck, it's working for a livelihood. I watched my parents work 16-hour days, every day. We had work to do when we came home from school, and it was a wake-up call and a lesson that most people don't understand.

"Mom would open the (package) store at 6 a.m. and close it at 10 p.m. Dad would drive for produce and then stock the store. I saw that, and it taught me a lot.

"No one wants to work. You have to work. You have to support your family. But it's not as difficult if you truly love what you do. If you love what you do, it's not a problem." His older brother, Ali, who now runs the menswear shop had a similar epiphany.

"All of us started the same way," said Ali Zabian. "We worked cleaning the building. We cleaned bathrooms, washed windows, vacuumed floors. I think my dad would have liked me to go into law or medicine, but I went to business school." When he graduated, Ali Zabian bought a business of his own, a dry cleaning establishment, from Paul Laramee. And though business was good, the nature of it was intense.

"I jumped in with both feet, and it was a great business, still is, but it just required so many people to run it properly. Paul Laramee had put a lot of work into it, and I owed it to his name to make sure it was in good hands."

He shopped for buyers and found a young Korean family who had the right connections to make it work. Once he'd handed over the staff, he returned to the fold.

"I really could appreciate this work. I could really see how it made a difference," Ali says of the store he grew up in. "We see teenagers who come for their first suits. Their first interview. College. Prom. I see how they go from jeans and tee to shirt and tie. I help dress them. They know me, and they trust me. The come here and they trust us. There is real joy and pride in that."

♥

Zabian's Fine Jewelers
www.zabians.com
Zabian's Clothing Ltd.
Mdouhka, Lebanon
www.mdoukha.org

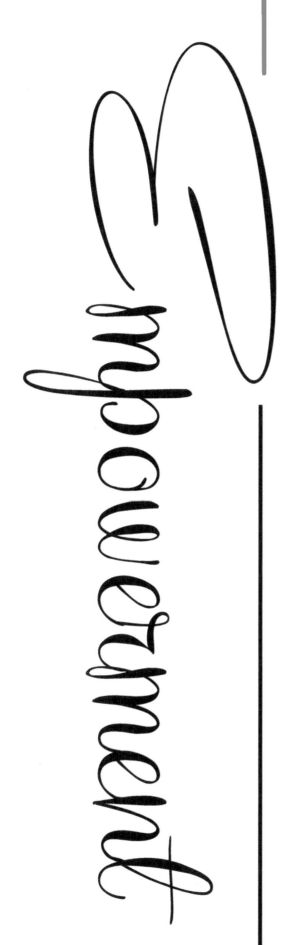

Empowerment

"I was going to die, sooner or later, whether or not I had even spoken myself. My silences had not protected me. Your silences will not protect you. What are the words you do not yet have? What are the tyrannies you swallow day by day and attempt to make your own until you will sicken and die of them, still in silence? We have been socialized to respect fear more than our own need for language. I began to ask each time, 'What's the worst that could happen to me if I tell this truth?' Unlike women in other countries, our breaking silence is unlikely to have us jailed, disappeared or run off the road at night. Our speaking out will irritate some people, get us called bitchy or hypersensitive and disrupt some dinner parties. And then our speaking out will permit other women to speak, until laws are changed and lives are saved and the world is altered forever. Next time, ask: What's the worst that will happen? Then push yourself a little further than you dare. Once you start to speak, people will yell at you. They will interrupt you, put you down and suggest it's personal. And the world won't end. And the speaking will get easier and easier. And you will find you have fallen in love with your own vision, which you may never have realized you had. And you will lose some friends and lovers, and realize you don't miss them. And new ones will find you and cherish you. And you will still flirt and paint your nails, dress up and party, because, as I think Emma Goldman said, 'If I can't dance, I don't want to be part of your revolution.' And at last you'll know with surpassing certainty that only one thing is more frightening than speaking your truth. And that is not speaking."

~Audre Lorde

BRIDGE Program Students at Pittsfield Public Schools

Maggie Adams & The Reverend Willard Durant

by Roberta Dews

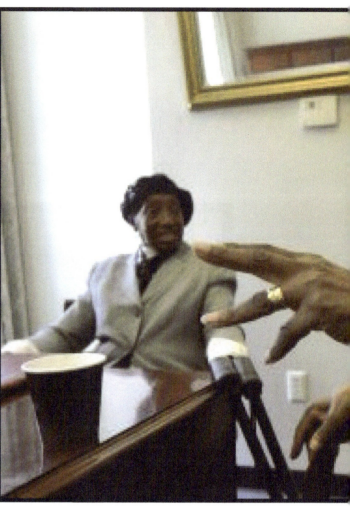

In 1980, the average cost of a house was $69,000; the median wage was $12,500, and a new car could cost about $7,200.

Fast-forward 32 years and things have most definitely changed. However, to Maggie Adams of Pittsfield, a former president of the NAACP chapter in the Berkshires, there will always be social issues that defy the test of time. This list includes combating discriminatory policies and behaviors in the housing and job markets, promoting equal education, and safeguarding the interests of veterans, she said.

"A group of us came together and found out what we needed to do," said Ms. Adams, who first became active with the NAACP as a teen in 1955 and led a reorganization of the group in 1980. "We were the watchdogs, and with the help of the national office we chose our focus. If someone felt they were discriminated in a job, we would write up that case and send it to the (Springfield) office, and if need be they will come to Pittsfield."

Today, the Berkshire NAACP chapter is inactive due to dwindled membership, but there is a growing effort to change that. An initial meeting was held this past March at the Second Congregational Church in Pittsfield and a second one on April 25. Through this process, Ms. Adams and others like the Reverend Willard Durant of Pittsfield, another past president, have been called upon to share their belief in the NAACP's relevance.

Despite the many past achievements of the group, which include protest marches against local lunch counters in the 1960s, successful voter reregistration drives and advocating for diverse product offerings in local stores, to name a few—the question of the chapter's relevance today is something both Ms. Adams and Reverend Durant say they've heard and readily counter.

"The fact of the matter is, you need a local voice," Reverend Durant said. "Some small group of people who can speak with authority. The NAACP is a very important tool." Ms. Adams adds that the NAACP works for change step by step, an approach that may frustrate those who want to see instant results.

The Berkshire NAACP was reactivated in December 2012

"We're dealing with a different generation," she said. "They're very short on patience." The NAACP's methods have gotten results in the past—and have appealed to a broad range of people. "The rules back then might have been old-fashioned, but it was fair play and (based on) unselfishness," Ms. Adams said. "There was an awareness and everyone was involved."

Top: with Anne Hampton, Bottom: with Gwendolyn Hampton VanSant

"...you need a local voice, some small group of people who can speak with authority. The NAACP is a very important tool."

Indeed, the Reverend points to the chapter's past objectives, which spurred a multicultural membership, a fact that many people today may not know about.

"The majority of the NAACP was white," said Reverend Durant, who was active with the group in the 1970s. "Some people know, but very few would actually say that was the case." Reverend Durant said that today's NAACP chapter should continue to reflect all people coming together for a common good. "You have to find out what the needs of the people are and that's not going to happen at the first meeting," he said. Ms. Adams also added that there might be a sentiment among some who don't want to involve outside agencies in their issues for fear of backlash.

"With the younger generation, they don't want to get anyone involved. They just want to leave it alone as it is. I say to them, *It's not [just] about you*." Because of his many years of work in our community he sends a message to the youth that should be heeded by all, "It's important for [you] to understand that change is a process."

♥

In Loving Memory of Willard Durant

In 2005 when Mohammed Adawulai, an exchange student from West Africa, came to meet his host family in the Berkshires, he brought with him a new suitcase with little in it. His most valuable possession was his desire for education.

"When you come to America you come to get something. You don't bring anything," he says. "I spent a couple of months trying to figure out where the Berkshires were in comparison to Boston or Washington." His progress these last few years has been nothing short of impressive. This past May, Mohammed graduated magna cum laude from Simon's Rock College and shared the commencement stage with Ben Bernanke, chairman of the Federal Reserve.

The 22-year-old from Kete-Krachi in the Volta region of Ghana credits PAX (Program for Academic Exchange), a designated Exchange Visitor Program by the U.S. Department of State, as contributing to his success. As well as the support of the school community and the perseverance of his host family.

After Ben Bernanke, the man Forbes Magazine has called the sixth most powerful in the world, finished his address which highlighted the optimism he saw for world economies, Mohammed stepped up to the podium to give his speech. With matched hopefulness for the contributions he and his fellow classmates will make during their careers, Mohammed implored them to mind the gaps.

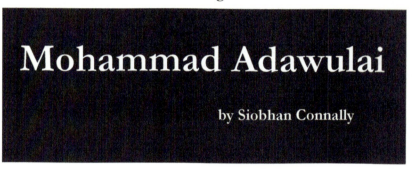

Mohammad Adawulai

by Siobhan Connally

"Increasingly, the gap between the global north and the global south has become wider. The poor nations keep getting poorer and the wealthy ones keep getting richer. Now I say this mindful of the fact that ultimately individuals and nations must take responsibility for themselves. But you do not need to be a rocket scientist to see that many of the world's poorest people are also the world's most hard working people. Hard work must be rewarded, but rewards that pay on the ability to create and maintain a system that is predicated on the enrichment of a few at the expense of many…such rewards are simply immoral. And this is only possible in a world that increasingly fails to recognize the shared destinies of its people," he said in his address.

Mohammed, who hopes to continue his studies of government policy, economics, and world affairs at the graduate level in Washington D.C. became interested in the gap between GDP indicators and real indicators of growth for individuals, and focused on those issues for his BA thesis.

He was particularly interested in the disconnect between national prosperity and regional and individual prosperity.

"Ghana is one of the five fastest growing economies in the world. We understand this because of its increase in investors in the region. But in reality it just doesn't add up. And you can say that about every nation. There are disparities between real growth and national growth.

"GDP is a measure that fluctuates based on investors and is reflected in national growth, but it doesn't tell the whole story." Mohammed's journey to the United States started in a classroom in Ghana, where he heard a teacher speak about the academic exchange organizations administered by the State Department.

"I had seen America on TV I knew I wanted to be there. I applied, took the exam and then had an interview. Thousands apply and I made it through the process." And then he had to tell his mother.

"It was a weird moment," he said. "I didn't tell my family about any of it. PAX called my uncle's phone to tell them I had been selected. It was easier to keep the bar low instead of raising their hopes." Ultimately, his parents were happy he'd been given the opportunity to go out into the world.

But even with rigorous preparation for students who will be traveling to new lands, as well as orientations for the host families who offer them shelter, the culture differences can be unsettling. For Mohammed, at first even minor things presented challenges.

Mohammad with JV Hampton-VanSant, BRIDGE Youth Coordinator

"When I first came I saw a huge divide between the way children are brought up here and the way they are brought up in Ghana. Some of my earliest experiences were as simple as not putting your arms around guys. [Many people} don't do that here."

"I didn't know anyone who identified (as gay or lesbian) before. I have met people from India, China, and Egypt. Naturally you find yourself challenged at first, coming from a community that is predominantly black to being immersed in a community that is so diverse. But as you begin to talk to people and get to know them you realize how much you have in common." Settling into family life was thorny at times. Mohammed lived with four families in five years.

"The families I met were good people, it just wasn't always smooth," he said. It's supposed to be challenging, and my goal was to treat them like my own parents. I think that's the key. Most of us expect difficulties, especially when it's all new. But I've learned a lot from those families and all of them came to my graduation."

The education system is different in Ghana, too. He says it lacks academic flexibility and relies more heavily on rote understanding. Students have to declare the career path they will take by the time they enter high school.

"In Ghana I was a science student. It wasn't my interest, but it was my aptitude. In the states, I took courses in politics and world affairs, and this is what I really want to do. Simon's Rock is a unique institution. It is deeply committed to academic excellence and the idea that you're thinking, and analysis is critical to promoting academic excellence," he said. "It's not about what you do, it's what you think about what you do that really matters."

LINKS:

Mohammed Adawulai's speech at Simon's Rock College's 44th commencement can be viewed in its entirety on YouTube at the Bard College at Simon's Rock channel

Poem gives Nakeida Bethel-Smith a voice and a place to stand. "It's a place of freedom," she said. "It's my world. However I envision it." She has written diaries since middle school or before, she said, and she found poetry as she found poets who seem to understand her life. Maya Angelou, Nikki Giovanni, and Lucille Clifton. She remembers the day she first read a poem by Nikki Giovanni.

"They spoke to me, as a black girl growing up," she said. They and writers of the Harlem Renaissance like Langston Hughes, Zora Neale Hurston, helped to give voice and perspective and wholeness to a girl raised not to interrupt when adults were talking. A girl whose mother would say, "speak up!"

"I'm loud and boisterous on my own," Bethel-Smith said, "but there are layers, everyone has layers, and poetry lets me uncover the layers in a transparent way. You can be whoever you want when you write." In poetry, she can be loud, even angry, she said. She can put aside the way women are often portrayed, any image of what women are "supposed to be" and she can speak the way she needs to speak. Women are often scared to be powerful, to command respect, she said. She calls for assertiveness with grace. And in poetry, she has found a way to speak up, and to help others to speak with her. Speaking aloud, she said, is a core part of poetry for her. Most poets read by themselves in coffee houses, she said. She got introduced to performance early on.

"I come alive on stage," she said. "I'm more nervous when I'm just reading. When I'm performing, I feel like another person." She named that performer Lady Nakeida, her slam-poetry alter-ego, and entrepreneurial, powerful self. Bethel-Smith started volunteering in the community when she was 19. She led a youth group at the Christian Center, she said, talking with kids only a few years younger than she was. She worked with the Women of Color Giving Circle and founded a community Kwanzaa celebration. And through the work she found a voice.

"I saw what I could do," she said. "Lady Nakeida grew out of that power."

That power has earned her recognition across and beyond the Berkshires, from a reading at yBar in this year's 10x10 Festival to a Senate Citation for 'Being named an up-and-coming young woman' in The Eagle. Last October, she performed her own work in Jerome Edgerton's original musical "The Evolution of Rhymes," with Barrington Stage Company, in a 1920s jazz set. She has also worked with playwright Jamuna Sirker, choreographer Marla Robertson and the young women in Shirley Edgerton's Rights of Passage group, and BSC actors, to create a performance from their own stories.

They will base their show around Ntozake Shange's, "For Colored Girls Who Have Considered Suicide When the Rainbow Is Enuf," a 1975 choreopoem performed on and

Nakeida Bethel-Smith

by Kate Abbott

off Broadway and on film. Shange will inspire their work, Bethel Smith said, and they will weave their stories together, she said, through dance, performance, poetry, and monologes.

"It's powerful to find a place where someone identifies with you," she said, "where you realize 'I'm not the only one who has been through this—I can share.'" The tools poetry has given her, and that she has gathered on her own, she hands on. As outreach educator at the Elizabeth Freeman Center, she speaks in schools and works with middle and high school students, talking about healthy relationships, sex education and ways to end teen violence and teen pregnancy.

> *"Faith is a skill that you have to practice, perserverance is an attitude."*

"Young people like truth," she said. "They will listen to truth if you don't tell them what *their* truth is. If you say, 'here are options, here is information. Now, what do you want to do?' She hopes to teach perseverance, "continuing to go on, no matter what your obstacles are."

"I was always the underdog," she said. "I found my own way. I can speak to the young person who doesn't have a voice or doesn't feel heard. Faith is a skill that you have to practice. Perseverance is an attitude." Confidence in herself, in her family and community, and in her God, lives at the core of her work. Nakeida serves as a minister at Price Memorial A.M.E. Church with the Reverend Walter Davis. The Reverend Willard Durant, a presence in the church for generations, is her spiritual grandfather, she said.

"As a minister, I help people understand that they have a purpose in their lives," she said. "We all minister to people; whether we're religious or not, we all want to encourage people and inspire them." She has felt since she was a child that she had something greater to do, she said, a sense of responsibility larger than herself.

"You feel a call," she said, "and then you make the decision that you want the call. I answered because I found a balance. I can be a minister and be Lady Nakeida, and work in the community."

She can appreciate Lady Nakeida's strength, and the compassion that she gives and finds in her work, and the people, the rare and valuable people, she can trust to take care of each other.

"People may be humbled but not humble—changed so that they value life," she said.

She will encourage people to think back to a time when someone took care of them, to help them think of giving that feeling to someone else.

"Every time I give," she said, "it takes another burden off of me."

Youlin Shi, a woman from China exclaims, "How much you discover as you write!" Along with new writer friends from Mexico, Japan, El Salvador, and Tashkent, she was preparing to read her immigration story in "Coming to America," a workshop sponsored by the Berkshire Immigrant Center in the Berkshire Women Writers Festival.

"This workshop helps us all understand the extraordinary challenges that immigrants face and appreciate freedoms we often take for granted," says Marge Cohan, Pittsfield resident, former director of the Brien Center, and Immigrant Center board member.

"Its wonderful diversity and collaborative spirit challenge common assumptions. Immigrant women from different cultures quickly establish universal connections. Multiculturalism, often associated with urban communities or border states, enriches our Berkshires. And Williams College's participation in this Festival represents a new, cross

county collaboration." The festival invited us all—writers, readers, audience members—to plumb our own stories, hear our own voices.

"The great American story," reflected Youlin, "is made of small stories like mine, which I want to share and pass on to the next generation. It's time now, in my life, to look back, see my footsteps, be sure my daughter understands how she happened to be born in the United States." Before and after they reach this country, many immigrants face danger— physical or psychological adversity, loss and/or despair. As in myths, action leads to agonizing, uncertain wandering, before new life, understanding, a better future emerges. Shi grew up during Mao's Cultural Revolution. Her father, a state official, was labeled an enemy of the party and held incommunicado for years, and she was sent to live and work in a village far from everyone she knew.

Crossing borders, parting from families, Marcela Villada Peacock, now a multi-cultural counselor at Williams left Mexico City years ago. "It was a long, scary time, not knowing the future. Fears linger," she acknowledged. "With my heart in two places, I enjoy helping people make this huge transition." Writing in English did not come easily to this group of women, trained in their native countries in engineering, education, history and economics.

"For whom are you writing?" asked workshop facilitator Greta Phinney, former Peace Corps volunteer and life-long teacher in Pittsfield, Latin America, and Africa.

"There were three answers," she said. "They want their children to know their stories. They want to connect with other women with whom they share universal life experiences. And they want the rest of us, not recent immigrants, to understand their lives. From the beginning, rich, powerful themes emerged."

When Milagros Diaz's parents left El Salvador for America, she was sent from the farm where she was born to live

Discovering America

by Margot Welch

with her grandparents. She stayed with them while she finished school and began teaching until she could to be reunited with her family. Feruza Bourn, an economist and researcher in Uzbekistan, left for freedom. She works now as a quality control technician in an automobile factory.

"In many ways, it was a journey to the unknown, goodbye to life as I knew it, everything that had always defined me." Said Esperanza, who requested that her real name not be used. She left Mexico City to marry an American and is now a graduate student.

"Slowly I've come to understand," Esperanza said, "that just like previous immigrants, with all our differences, we help shape what the U.S. is today and will be tomorrow. This is what the American dream means to me."

"I have realized that America is not a perfect society," says Youlin, a historian now teaching Tai-chi and cooking. "But compared to some countries where your life, even your thinking, is dictated by the state, this country recognizes the inalienable rights of her citizens. It is like holding the key to your own house."

While every story is different, all the women have been subject to exploitation, stigmatization, and wrenching loneliness. Now, though, they treasure discovering how much they have in common. Finding their voices, they are not alone. Exuberance sang out in Midori's voice, a Japanese woman who was gratefully writing herself away from past trauma, as it did in Milagros excitement. "Now, no matter what happens," she says, "I want to continue learning until I die!"

> "Once we realize how short is our tenure on the planet earth, telling stories helps us to see."

"Once we realize how short is our tenure on the planet earth," said Greta, "telling stories helps us to see."

We're all explorers from some other land or time. Wherever our journeys have taken us, with memory and imagination, we can make sense of where we've been. In the end, what's extraordinary is discovery of ourselves, others, and the richness of every life lived, spoken, and on the page.

Sarah Gillooly

by Kate Abbott

Five to nine-year-old girls get excited all through the school year for time outside to relax and feel safe, to get away from phones and devices, walk in the woods, get dirty, swim in the lake, play games in the fields and make art in the cabins.

"I can't wait," they tell Sarah Gillooly, Girls Inc Program/Camps Director at the Gladys Allen Brigham Community Center. She runs a girls-only day camp in the summer on Onota Lake in Pittsfield, and she shares her campers' excitement.

"It's an experience many of them won't get otherwise," she said. As the child of a single mother, she understands the opportunities not all children have. "When I was growing up, we didn't have a canoe," she said. "We didn't know anyone who had a canoe."

Some students come to summer camp and become counselors and work for the center in their late teens. The Brigham Center also offers programs year-round for children, boys and girls, from infants to teenagers. "We have had people from infant and toddler to 13 or 14," she said.

Away from the lake, Sarah teaches programs for older girls through the Brigham Center and local schools with the national organization, Girls Inc. She has cared about girls and equality, she said, as long as she can remember.

"My mother always told me I could do anything and be anything I wanted to," she said. "School was huge for me. I remember being young and not wanting to disappoint her."

Her mother had faced stiff challenges to give her daughter this confidence. Sarah said her mother had left college and divorced young, and she had broken her neck in a diving accident and was paralyzed from the neck down. She gave her daughter a firm foundation. Sarah recalls her childhood with thankful warmth and respect.

She studied sociology at Simmons College. "It's not a girl's school without men—it's a women's college without boys," she said, smiling, "and you're in Boston."

She volunteered in Boston with CityYear, an international nonprofit bringing education to communities where people need it. Then she came back to the Berkshires to reach out to communities here.

At Pittsfield High School, she said, girls can choose to join the Girls Inc. programs instead of gym. She offers "Taking Care of Business," teaching pregnancy prevention, sex education, and the power and consequences a choice can have.

"We say, *make a life for yourself before you make another life*," she said.

With other girls, students can feel safe and able to ask questions, she added, sometimes more than in a co-ed group.

Girls Inc. offers a range of programs to schools that approach the Brigham Center. An economic program teaches real-world skills: how to apply for a job, save and get to college, invest, pay taxes. A math and science course encourages girls to learn about women who work in these fields. Media literacy helps girls think about the advertising and images they see every day online, on television and in print.

"They face a lot of social pressure, media pressure and peer pressure," she said. "Kids are so attached to their devices."

Her students often struggle with their peers and friends, she said. Someone may act like a friend one day and not the next.

"I have a 13-year-old niece," she said. "For adolescent girls, friendship and bullying and teasing are huge, whether it's in your face or on some form of media. Trying to fit in or trying to be your own person and not fit in, what does that mean?" It takes confidence for them to stand up for themselves and for other people.

S.A.Y. It Proud award winner, Shakia Green

"My mother used to say *think before you speak*," she said. "Your voice is a powerful tool." She reminds herself that she does not always know what struggles her students face outside of the classroom. Sometimes their lives are chaos, and chaos is what they know. She hopes to help them recognize the choices they have.

She speaks from her own experience when she tells the girls she teaches, "You can do this if you work hard enough. You are not your past. This doesn't have to be all you ever do, all you ever know."

Girls Inc. also teaches self-defense and violence prevention programs for girls ages 6 to 8, 9 to 11 and 12 to 14. She teaches 9 to 11-year-olds self-defense skills, ways to handle teasing and bullying and manage anger, and tools to prevent or cope with sexual assault.

Her students learn to break a board, and they demonstrate their skill at the end of the class—and they get to keep their board. Many tell her years later they still have their boards, she said. She has hers in her office.

> *"If you don't have goals, how can you go farther than where you are? A goal is a dream with a deadline."*

She has taught these programs since 1999, and in all that time she has also worked with the Elizabeth Freeman Center, helping survivors of domestic and sexual violence and their families. She serves as a rape crisis counselor and answers the hotline, she said, works as an advocate and acts as a teacher here too, working with the adults at the center to help them get their lives back.

At the Brigham Center, she works with younger girls to expand their lives.

"If you don't have goals, how can you go farther than where you are?" she said. "A goal is a dream with a deadline."

The center encourages girls to think about what they like to do and how they can turn their likes [into a career] they would love, she said. She wants her students to understand that a career can be something to love. She loves her own. She loves feeling she has made a difference, kicking back by the lake in casual clothes, having a student say, *I can't wait for camp."*

"Knowing they look forward to it means the world to me," she said.

Saidiya Hartman is a professor at Columbia University who lives in the Berkshires in the summer and returns to New York City for the rest of the year. On one of her visits to the local transfer station in the town of Monterey, Massachusetts, she had a conversation with a woman with whom she had something in common.

"[She] went to the same high school as I did, Christ the King in Queens, New York. It's a small world in those ways."

Though this was an unexpected bond in an unusual setting, Saidiya has focused on the idea of commonalities in recent years. It began when she traveled to Ghana in 1998. She stayed for a year to learn more about the stories of those affected by the Atlantic Slave Trade, but she ended up writing a more personal story based on her mother's ancestral roots in Ghana. She documented this experience in a 2007 book, *Lose Your Mother: A Journey Along the Atlantic Slave Route*.

"I think people, we create our identities, so I think there's power in that....How and where we belong, that's not static. It changes."

She had to rethink notions of shared experiences among the peoples of the African diaspora and learned to broaden her meanings of identity and community in a global world.

But disclosing these revelations came with a cost, she said. "People have very strong feelings about *Lose Your Mother*. Some people liked it, but some hated it because it talked about the tensions between African-Americans and Africans," she said. "And then there was my mother; she was upset because she felt exposed in a way. It was like, *Why do you have to talk about your family at all?*" Turning the attention toward her family wasn't the initial plan.

Saidiya's visit to Ghana was for a research project, but when she was hindered by a lack of archived material, she was left with little to move forward. "I was struggling with the lack of firsthand accounts. I asked myself, *How am I going to write a book about an encounter with nothing?*" she said. Her many specializations include African-American history.

"It was the other scholars I was with who said, *This story is very personal. Stop resisting.*" Reviewing the detailed journal she kept during her stay in Ghana, she saw her story come alive on the pages. "I had hundreds of pages of my experiences, enabling me to reflect on the scholarly and the personal," she said. One of the main issues centered on her identity as a black American in relation to the Ghanaians.

"I didn't feel like I was an outsider; people were telling me I was an outsider. They called me 'bruni,' which means white person, or stranger or westerner," she said. The term is used interchangeably. But for Saidiya, even trying to talk about slavery was considered an affront at times.

"I expected there to be a similar reaction to slavery in West Ghana as it was in the diaspora, but there was such a different take on it. It was like, why would you bring (slavery) up," said Saidiya, who also spent some time in Curaçao learning about her dad's roots. "Plus, there was African slavery; it was like these two histories of slavery that were overlapping. There's shame that Africans have for participating as trade partners with Europeans. We don't ingest how complicated that legacy is."

Photo from US Slave Blog

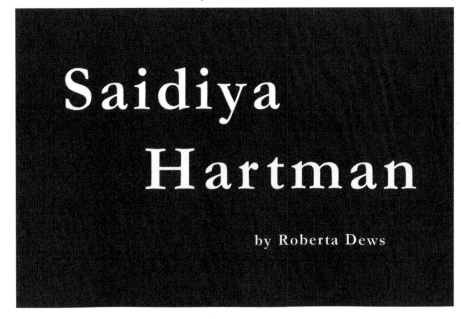

Saidiya Hartman

by Roberta Dews

Interestingly, Hartman found that the longing she had for an ancestral home that, in essence, no longer recognized her as one of its own, was a theme that resonated with others. "Some people identified with how we've been shaped by the past.

Also, it was interesting to speak with a European immigrant who said it felt like I was telling her story about a home that no longer exists," she said. "People who experienced homelessness and displacement also identified with it."

Reconciled with her past and history, Saidiya's identity today is, in a way, fluid.

"I think people, we create our identities, so I think there's power in that. I guess I would say that that was part of my journey," she said. "How and where we belong, that's not static. It changes."

Karran Larson

by Margot Welch

Karran Larson loves being deaf and she means every word. But it hasn't always been so. A case manager for the Massachusetts Commission for the Deaf and Hard of Hearing (MCDHH), Karran was born in a small Illinois town in the early 1950s. Long before newborn screenings and rubella vaccinations were routine, Karran's mother was concerned.

"You worry too much," the pediatrician said. "She's just a little slow. She'll outgrow it." In school, Karran sat in the first row, observing her teachers vigilantly. Never hearing the bell, she told herself someday she'd understand how all the kids knew exactly when to put their papers away and get up to leave the classroom. Her teachers, calling her lazy and inattentive, recommended she be put into a state institution for the retarded. Fortunately, a second grade teacher said, "That child isn't dumb! She needs a hearing test!"

The only deaf member of her family, Karran found her home supportive, attentive and loving. Her father, an ardent civil rights activist, insisted on the importance of reading, which developed Karran's linguistic capacity.

"He made good rules," she recalled. "At dinner we all sat around a circular dining table. I could see everybody when they spoke. Only one person was allowed to talk at a time, never with a mouth full!" Except for middle school years at the Central Institute for the Deaf in St. Louis, where she learned lip-reading and speech, Karran attended regular schools.

In the late 1960s, when Civil Rights, Women's Liberation, and Deaf and Disability Pride initiatives were changing the world, Karran enrolled at the University of Southern Illinois. She then transferred to the New School for Social Research in New York City, and got a master's degree in rehabilitation counseling from New York University.

"The times were so powerful," she said. "It used to be that I had a 'hearing problem.' Even with my wonderful family, I grew up without a deaf role model or deaf peers, internalizing an unspoken message from the dominant culture that part of me was defective. I needed to fake it. But then, meeting healthy, unashamed deaf people, I was out! I didn't care what anyone thought. With Deaf Pride, everything changed. I'm so proud to be a part of the deaf community."

> *"I grew up without a deaf role model or deaf peers. But then, meeting healthy, unashamed deaf people, I was out! I didn't care what anyone thought."*

Now bilingual in English and American Sign Language (ASL) and knowledgeable about the lifeways of deaf people, Karran was becoming bicultural. She loved living in New York, but not wanting to raise children there, moved with her family to the Berkshires. Discovering a significant need for mental health counseling among deaf students, she transferred to the Massachusetts Department of Mental Health in Pittsfield, becoming a licensed mental health counselor. Now, with her colleagues, she supplemented her individual counseling with the critical work of interagency collaboration. Thriving on challenges, Karran spends much of her time advocating, counseling, referring, consulting, training, and improving cooperation among various state departments such as, Health, Developmental Disabilities, Mental Health, Education, Justice, Housing, Transitional Assistance, and Legal Assistance. One aspect of her work involves helping growing numbers of deaf immigrants. Many have special educational needs and may be victims of violence, mentally or physically ill, in need of housing or legal assistance, she said. Arriving here, they may know their country's distinctive sign language. But some, deaf from birth, may never have learned to sign. The degree to which linguistic capacity develops will depend on a child's age when hearing is lost. In refugee camps, Karran adds, medical care, like schooling, is minimal. Knowing American Sign Language helps deaf immigrants to take part in resettlement and citizenship programs.

"*I'm so proud to be a part of the deaf community.*"

"Where there is ESL, there should be ASL," Karran insisted. Significant comprehension and communication difficulties make it hard to find work, she said. This is true for all immigrants. And if they do not understand what is expected of them to comply with visa requirements, their lives are shadowed with deportation fears.

"I'm a high-energy person," Karran said. "My work keeps me challenged. It's good."

Conveying the joy she finds in life, Karran also understands the scorn and disrespect that anyone learning a new culture may experience. Devoting herself to alleviating the isolation and practical needs of the deaf, this generous, experienced, gifted woman is also a human-rights advocate. Questioning, making connections, and, like her father, pushing for change, Karran enriches all cultures lucky enough to claim her as a member.

The obituary for a man who died in 1982 at the age of at 92 is yellowed and cut slightly unevenly out of a newspaper. It tells of the life of the early Italian immigrant, Ralph J. Rotondo Sr. who came to the U.S in 1908, when he was about 19. He worked on railroad construction in Geneva, New York, for a few years, sending money back to his family in Italy, choosing to live leanly. On a visit to his mother in Italy, he was drafted into the Italian army and served in North Africa for a few years before returning to settle in Lee.

His son, Ralph Rotondo Jr. said his father never returned to Italy again. He had a disagreement with his only sister when she visited Lee, and he cut ties with his family overseas. Ralph Sr. worked at Lee Marble, making steam to run the cranes. He then worked at Eagle Mill as a fireman, firing the steam room to power the mill.

Ralph Rotondo

by Kuukua Dzigbordi Yomekpe

He studied for his engineer's license to become a steam engineer and worked at a tannery, where he was promoted to fireman and stayed until the place went out of business.

Ralph Jr. speaks fondly of his father, who instilled his work ethic by making sure he got a job the minute school let out each summer. Ralph Jr. said he loved horses and was delighted to find work as a farm hand, where he learned to ride and drive carts. He worked at the paper mill in Lee as a day-time job for 37 years, but his love of horses led him to purchase horses for his five daughters. He was unhappy with the local farrier, the man who forged horseshoes and shod horses in the neighborhood and he learned how to shoe horses himself. When others noticed he was doing this, they asked him to do their horses. When professional farrier, Clarence Martin of Sheffield, who learned to shoe horses during the war, saw his handiwork he asked him to be his apprentice.

Ralph Jr. smiled as he told how, at the end of his one-year apprenticeship, the farrier split the payment for a job with him, telling him he was good enough to go out on his own. What had started as his attempt to do a better job grew into a business, and Ralph Jr. traveled throughout New England to shoe race horses and even the Budweiser Clydesdales. He said the harnesses for Budweiser horses were made in the gray building next to the present-day Briarcliff Motel. He kept shoeing until he was about 79. Then he trimmed shoes until he retired at 81. He and his wife still keep a pony on their farm in Lee. His wife, Jeannette, whose mother emigrated from Quebec, also grew up loving horses.

The couple met at Jeannette's uncle's house, according to their daughter, Donna. Ralph had come for a meeting—he rode with Jeannette's uncle in the Powder River Riding Club in 1953.

> *"It was always amazing to see [my dad] and his horses pulling different apparatuses in parades and events."*

Jeannette taught people how to ride and care for horses and then build trust in them. She enjoyed working with young people, she said, especially those with special needs. She still teaches her great grandchildren, though the Rotondos no longer give lessons or carriage rides. Their eyes lit up as they took turns talking about their carriage business. Besides shoeing, showing and grooming horses, they discovered the tradition of carriage parades. Jeannette believed the tradition began in the early 1900s, when wealthy women paraded up and down Main Street, all dressed up and riding in horse-drawn carriages. The Rotondo's got involved in showing horses and carriages in various town fairs and festivals, like the Colonial Carriage and Driving, Tub Parade, and Norman Rockwell Christmas. They spoke with excitement about their favorite and most expensive carriage, white with maroon velvet interior, which they bought for $4,000.

"It was always amazing to see [my dad] and his horses pulling different apparatuses in parades and events," Donna said. "He took my son to the prom in his white carriage, and he was the last one to get a ride in that." They provided horses and carriages for the proms of four of their five grandchildren. They turned the carriages into a side business and did local weddings. Donna remembers when Town & Country magazine did a bridal shoot with the Rotondo carriages and horses and Ralph in his tuxedo. Jeannette nods and speaks a quote by Winston Churchill they have used as a guiding principle throughout their years of working with horses, "There is something about the outside of a horse that is good for the inside of a man."

Jeannette and Ralph Rotondo

The Reverend Shelia Sholes-Ross is currently at the start of her second year ministering to the congregation of the First Baptist Church in Pittsfield. She is the 30th senior pastor of the church, having relocated to the Berkshires with her husband, Nelson Ross, on January 23, 2014. Both come from New Orleans and spent a couple of decades living and working near Durham, North Carolina. While Sholes-Ross first heard her calling to God early on in life, it's only been in recent years that she has been firmly rooted in the ministry.

"I heard [a calling] at 17 years old but never seeing an African American female clergy person where I grew up, I didn't think [I could do] it," she said. By 1978, she had two bachelor's degrees, and she went on to earn a master's in administration and supervision, and then a master's in public health, before finally understanding this calling and pursuing a divinity degree.

"Before I felt the calling to God, I felt the calling to advocacy." She said her first act of advocacy and foray into feminism, got her kicked out of her Girl Scouts Brownies troop. "I didn't like just baking cookies," she said. "I wanted to find out why the boys in the Cub Scouts were doing something different than we were. I wanted to be a part of that too."

> "I know that God has called me here, not just to be a pastor of First Baptist but to make a difference in the community."

She attributes much of her will and character development to her mother, Ruth Nicholas Sholes. "She was a trailblazer." In the early 1900s, her mother marched into a bank and negotiated a loan, becoming a hairdresser and owner of her own beauty salon.

"I always had a strong woman in my life," Sholes-Ross said, "and since I was a little girl, I've always advocated on behalf of all women." As the first female and first African-American leader of the First Baptist Church in Pittsfield, the Reverend Sholes-Ross isn't afraid to state, "Yes, this is history."

Her own identity and ownership of that fact doesn't mean she's only an advocate for people or women like her. "We are in this together," she said. "I'm not just going to advocate on behalf of black women or women of color…and that's the struggle with women, we don't work on behalf of one another."

Fortunately, she has a strong ally; her husband of 27 years, who was willing to pack up his successful career and venture with her to New England. "I'm a blessed woman. He's not intimidated by my success, and he's an advocate for females too. I am so proud of that."

Beyond her work in the church and towards raising the

The Reverend greets young parishioner

The Reverend Sheila Sholes-Ross

by Jenn Smith

The Reverend greets her parishioners after Sunday service

status of women, she's also demonstrated that's she's ready to roll up her sleeves and go to bat for our city. "I know that God has called me here, not just to be a pastor of First Baptist but to make a difference in the community," she said. One of the first appointments she made was with Pittsfield Police Chief Michael Wynn, not at a desk, but in a four-hour ride along with him in a police cruiser through every back alley and byway.

"We can't do this alone, and we need all the help we can get," Chief Wynn said during Reverend Sholes-Ross's formal installation celebration last August. Reverend Sholes-Ross now serves as one of the adult members of the recently revived Pittsfield Youth Commission. She brings to the table her experience working with high-school dropout populations and as past executive director of Communities in Schools in Orange County, North Carolina. She's also partnered with Rabbi Josh Breindel of Temple Anshe Amunim in a number of collaborations, including hosting a joint service to commemorate Martin Luther King Jr. Day.

She's working to develop youth ministry and outreach through her church, she said, and to reach out to other underserved populations, like people who struggle with mental health issues and things like housing and food insecurity.

"You shouldn't be made to feel like an outcast when you're struggling," she said. "I try to meet with people, to see where the greatest need is and how I can fit in to help." She works to stay actively involved in the community she's still learning about. To keep her energy, stamina and focus on her missions of ministry and empowerment, she said it's also important to "make time for Sheila," to help find clarity and stay on task.

"I have my days." She said. "Things have not always been easy." She hit multiple glass ceilings in her effort to find a congregation that would accept her. "I was denied 33 times as pastor," she said.

She relied on inner strength and support from friends and loved ones until First Baptist in Pittsfield found her. "We have to take care of ourselves physically and emotionally," she said. "I want to ensure I'm able to be everything I can be. Every day I get up and spend time with God. I exercise and then come [to the church] to see what's on the plate. God will put me where I need to be."

In case she needs a reminder, Proverbs 3:5-6 is displayed on her desk: "Trust in the Lord with all your heart and lean not on your own understanding; in all your ways acknowledge him, and he will make your paths straight."

Will Amado Syldor-Severino

by Siobhan Connally

Will Amado Syldor-Severino is holding his three-week-old son, Abi. The jobs counselor and community activist is a senior fellow with Americorps Massachusetts Promise and plans to return to his studies in social justice at the conclusion of his fellowship. "I wear this hat every day," he says, of his baseball hat, which depicts the Ejército Zapatista de Liberación Nacional flag (EZLN). "The way the Zapatistas in Mexico do organizing has been really inspirational for me. They, above most organizations, show me that this work can be done in a loving way and that talking—talking can not only destroy things but also rebuild."

It's blessedly quiet as Will checks on his newborn. His son, Abi, is three weeks old and sleeping peacefully as we chat. "He's a good baby," he says with a smile, answering my question about new-parent exhaustion. Ordinarily, though, for Will silence isn't golden. Silence is suspect. Will is one of the eleven scholars featured in StirFry Seminars' latest documentary 'If These Halls Could Talk,' filmed in 2010 and released last year. The film, by acclaimed director Lee Mun Wah, discusses diversity on college campuses across the country and the painful issues that are often left unsaid. "It took me a while to realize it, but racism exists in a way that is unique to this county. The silence says more than the words."

Now a senior fellow with Americorps Mass Promise working locally as a jobs and careers counselor with The Railroad Street Youth Project, Will has focused on implementing a more holistic approach when assisting students as they transition toward young adulthood.

"It's more than just resumes and how a person dresses. It's also about identity and how that impacts their lives. It's not just about getting in, it's about recognizing your own value as a worker and what importance you bring with you. I want people to see themselves as workers with value."

Admittedly, it's been a tough job. One that he's been taking day by day. "It's been harder and harder to feel as if the work I'm doing is sustainable," he worries. "I've seen people talk about moving forward in terms of social justice, but then racial politics does just the opposite. For instance, in the way budgets are prioritized or how initiatives in racial justice and social justice politics go nowhere. It seems as if racism is seen as an issue that can be put on the back burner." What he wants to feel is not only support in these endeavors but also a sense of urgency.

"What I found to be important is bringing people of color together and having them feel more affirmed in their experiences, and that they can speak to whom they are and what they've gone through, especially for young people. I'd like to see more unification across the county. I'd like to see more opportunity for people to be connected to each other." His own passion for social justice came as a result of his own upbringing in Brockton, and also from searching his own intolerances later in life.

"I think coming through Brockton and going to church with my folks seeing different people from different places gave me a different perspective. In college, I became aware of a variety of things that were happening on campus. I think I became interested in many social justice causes because I was aware of myself. My own ways of viewing the world were really skewed—racist and sexist and heterosexist—I wanted to be honest with myself, and I felt uncomfortable around an openly gay man. When I recognized I was dehumanizing a woman just because she was a woman, and the way I assumed the stupidity of a poor person because they were poor. I knew that for my own self-preservation and my own self-worth I needed to figure out what was going on and how these processes affected society and led to violence and destruction." Ultimately, however, Will believes that the hard conversations can't be left unexplored.

"It's about creating a space for this conversation," explains Will, who notes that while it is important to have gatherings that celebrate diverse cultures through food, music or other forms of artistry, it's not enough. "We need to have real conversations about race that are different from what people are used to," he said, adding that only when people work through the toxic emotions—the rage, anger, bitterness and fear—will they come to a place of healing.

> *"What I found to be important is bringing people of color together and having them feel more affirmed in their experiences..."*

"The only way to really ensure survival and a positive life is to struggle. I care about my kid, I care about [his] children and the communities children and there's no other way to ensure their safety besides struggling to make that a reality. To really shed a light on the deep impact on these isms (sexism, racism, and classism) has on society."

A 2012 graduate of UMass with a degree in English, Will has plans to continue his studies in social justice at the graduate level.

For more information about StirFry Seminars, visit www.stirfryseminars.com

It's never easy growing up feeling different. For many lesbian, gay, bisexual or transgender (LGBT) teens, in addition to feeling different, they often feel disaffected and detached. Pittsfield native Jason Verchot remembers feeling the same as a youth.

"I came out when I was 18 and didn't know anyone in school or anywhere that was gay. Being gay wasn't something people talked about. I didn't actually tell my parents that I was gay, they kind of suspected, but telling them was the easy part. The difficult part was coming out to everyone else. I came out to a select group of trusted friends, and I didn't really tell anyone else," said Jason, who also serves as board president of the Berkshire Stonewall Community Coalition.

Trusting a close knit group of supporters is a common theme among LGBT people. In fact, many supporting organizations encourage waiting until the age of 18 to officially come out, yet research suggests that the age of "coming out" has been dropping in recent years. Easier access to information and widespread availability of support services for LGBT youth, such as those provided by Berkshire Stonewall, have provided greater opportunities for socialization and self-affirmation. Yet it wasn't until after he graduated from high school and enrolled at Berkshire Community College that things seemed to change for Jason.

> *It's never easy growing up feeling different. For many LGBT teens, in addition to feeling different they often feel disaffected and detached.*

"[By that time] I didn't really care what people thought," he said. "I dressed how I wanted, and it was quite obvious to everyone that I was gay. Then I went to the University of Massachusetts and found a great community there. It was an entirely different experience." After graduating from UMass, he stayed in Amherst for a while before returning to Pittsfield.

"At first, I was reluctant to come home. I just didn't want to leave [that environment] and my safety net of friends," he said. "But when I did, I noticed that things had changed. Downtown had changed with more of a focus on the arts, and

Jason Verchot

by JV Hampton-VanSant & Nik Davies

I think it made it easier to find acceptance in this area." Going back to Berkshire Stonewall was a natural progression for him. "I'd been a part of the organization since I was 17 as a member of their youth group," he said. "I became a member of the board about seven years ago."

Berkshire Stonewall was incorporated in 1997. Their mission is to promote the well-being of gay, lesbian, bisexual and transgender people of the Berkshires. How they've done that has changed throughout the years depending upon needs. Today, they focus on getting information to the high schools and forming Gay-Straight Alliances (GSA).

"[At Berkshire Stonewall] we provide people with things to do and a safe environment so they can be comfortable being 'out' amongst people who they know aren't judging them," Jason said. "But we find that people still feel that they are being judged on certain levels."

The National Coalition of Anti-Violence Projects released a collective report in May of 2013 on hate crimes against LGBTQ people. It noted that despite increased public and political acceptance of gays and lesbians, the number of crimes against LGBTQ people is the highest since 1998. The amount of physical violence, rather than just verbal abuse, has also skyrocketed, and, not surprisingly, younger people, transgender people and people of color are targeted the most and are twice as likely as their peers to say they have been physically assaulted, kicked or shoved at school. For LGBT youth around the world, "fear is part of their daily lives. Fear of their parents finding out. Fear of rejection or of being thrown out of the house. For parents, it's the fear of rejection from their peers. It's fear in the workplace that they can't talk freely about a gay, lesbian, bi or trans loved one. Everyone should be able to live free of fear," says Jody Huckaby, executive director of Parents, Families and Friends of Lesbians and Gays (PFLAG)."

> "All we can do is keep working to get things in an even better place for the next generation..."

Thanks to organizations such as Berkshire Stonewall, there has been a positive change regarding public feelings toward LGTB people in Berkshire County. There is also help and support to be found for LGBT teens, parents, and their supporters. "Today, it is a much different thing to be gay in Berkshire County," Jason said.

When asked what words of support he would give to youth struggling with an LGTB identity, he had this to say: "I tend to go back to that old cliché, 'It gets better.' The world they live in is different than the world that I lived in, and is certainly different than the generation before me. All we can do is keep working to get things in an even better place for the next generation until the day comes when it won't even matter if we're gay or straight or whatever it is we want to be."

Author & Editor-in-Chief Bios

♥

Gwendolyn Hampton VanSant is a Berkshire County resident and community organizer as well as CEO and Founding Director of Multicultural BRIDGE, an organization putting the Berkshires on the map for embracing diversity in a rural community and engaging in tough conversations around race and equity throughout our region. Under her leadership in design and implementation, BRIDGE is cited by social psychologists and criminal justice professors as a unique, effective model for community building, cultural proficiency training and reduction of hate crime for all communities--both urban and rural and everything in between. The work has been proven evidence-based with positive results and is cited in criminal justice textbook, *Understanding Hate Crimes*, by Carolyn Petrosino (Routeledge 2015).

Gwendolyn is a certified Spanish language interpreter for medical and mental health. She holds certificates in Positive Psychology (Wholebeing Institute at Kripalu), Diversity Leadership (NCBI), Autism Training (Options Institute) and more topics related to engaging families of diverse backgrounds. Gwendolyn designs highly customized programs for all of her clients. She also serves as appointed state official in the capacity of Chair of the Berkshire County Commission on the Status of Women. Gwendolyn serves on the Berkshire Chamber of Commerce and the Board of Visitors at Miss Hall's School. She is on the original steering committee for Lift Ev'ry Voice, An African American Festival in the Berkshires, and also on the Reactivation Committee of the Berkshire County NAACP. She has served on the African American Heritage Trail as well. She is mostly known for the creation and growth of Multicultural BRIDGE, which now serves in Vermont, across Massachusetts and in to New York State. She works passionately to advocate for her family and to incorporate positive psychology and authentic leadership in all of her work.

♥

Nik Davies has written children's literature since she was a child herself. Throughout the years, she has developed a love for every aspect of the publishing process from first words to the final literary product. She has published articles and columns in Berkshires Week & the Shires of Vermont and Berkshire Family Focus and is the author and publisher of children's books including her own young adult dystopian thriller, Fif15teen. She is a native New Yorker that has lived and travel throughout the country and world.

Nik serves on the Board of the Berkshire United Way and as Vice President of Governance on the Multicultural BRIDGE Board of Directors. She has also served as a Diversity Committee Member for Eversource Energy.

She is mostly known for her outrageous sense of humor, her eclectic style and her love for giving back to the community. She's a graphic designer, artist, editor, author, mother and wife. She lives in Massachusetts, with her family.

♥

Reflections from our Contributing Writers

♥

Kate Abbott - It began for me in January 2012 when Gwendolyn Hampton VanSant, founder of Multicultural BRIDGE and a person I had long wanted to meet, arranged a showing and discussion of the PBS documentary series called 'RACE–The Power of Illusion' at the Beacon Cinema in Pittsfield. On three January nights at the local movie house, I watched this three-part series and stayed for the group discussion afterward. For all the years I have lived in the Berkshires, I knew almost none of the other participants by sight. I began then to learn of Gwendolyn's genius for knowing people, and for bringing them together. That evening Gwendolyn and I discussed the idea of giving people a place for their voices to be heard. These profiles from On the BRIDGE, this *Berkshire Mosaic* is that place.

In Pittsfield, in the reviving center of our New England mill city, we have Malaysian, Vietnamese, Chinese and Japanese, Mexican and Eastern European, Italian and Indian restaurants. We have a West African market, and the teenagers waiting at the crosswalk are teasing each other in Spanish. Our Police Chief is African-American and Polish. Telling stories from many backgrounds matters to me.

So many generous people have talked with me; they have told me what they were homesick for. They have fed me bean soup with bacalao. This connectedness is an energy and a magic. It's Rabbi Josh Breindel singing the Dayenu from Temple Anshe Amunim's Passover service and Kori Alston glowing with the memory of playing Henry V at Shakespeare & Company. It's Grace and Luis Guerrero talking about reconnecting after his 22-day drive from here to Ecuador, and it's Gabriela Cruz telling me about celebrating Las Posadas in Oaxaca.

One night over dinner, Nik Davies told us about the day she offered a friendly acquaintance an apple, and he told her that he was fasting for Ramadan. When they got talking about the holiday, he told her that Ramadan was a time to pay attention; it wasn't a time to give things up, but to see and touch them more clearly. Driving home later, Nik said she saw the familiar road in a new light. I hope we have done as much for anyone who listens and talks with us.

Kate Abbott has been Berkshires Week editor at The Berkshire Eagle since 2008. Her magazine, presently called Berkshires Week and Shires of Vermont, has grown and now spans into Vermont. In her search for things to do and see for her section, she has wandered from farms to dance studios, felt the texture of gold leaf, vaulted on horseback and listened to Emily Dickinson in a hay barn on a summer night. She earned her MFA in fiction at the University of New Hampshire, and she has had poetry published in literary magazines including the Comstock Review and Entelechy International. She enjoys talking with people, walking in the woods, playing the recorder, and writing stories about all three.

♥

Liz Blackshine - Offerings of underrepresented cultures in our community are given a public, artful platform through the unique collaboration between Multicultural BRIDGE and the Berkshire Eagle. There is nothing like the moment I greet a stranger, am welcomed into their world, and taken down their memory lane, maybe the slow lane, perhaps an express lane, or a winding and usually bumpy path to the center, their center, where their heart finds its beat. You could say I'm in love with the spark I see in a person when they connect the happenings of their lives with what they feel compelled to offer to the community.

I'll let you in on a little secret: I confess, newspaper writing is not my passion. It's the interviewing that does it for me. As a columnist for On the BRIDGE I've been on such adventures as to discover the juicy roots underneath a local biannual summer long African American arts festival, a teenage girl's youth leadership to resolve multicultural conflict in her high school, a small alternative school's joyous and skillful perpetuation of pagan rituals and celebrations, local youth making reality of Dr. Martin Luther King Jr.'s visions in our community, an academic couple's lifelong pursuit of researching and sharing the history of oppressed peoples in this country, a local pastor's contagious vibrancy and long served purpose to advocate for gay and civil rights throughout the Northeast and help all peoples of faith to become the miracles we long for. The opportunity to research, commune with and ultimately share these people's stories was an adventure I am proud and humbled to have traveled this last year.

One of my favorite quotes from these interviews is from African American Professor and Chair of the Dance Department at Williams College, Sandra Burton. Burton says what I sense I hear in the heartbeat of all the interviews: "Being fluent, being comfortable with other people is a survival skill. These are the tools for helping people communicate and learn how to live in the same time-space continuum with each other. There's a reason we have image making, why we have fashion, why we sing, why we go on the stage, why we have stories. They are the fabric all human beings hold onto."

I'll end with a prayer I offered in one of my blogs: "May we continue to share our own personal stories on faith and spirituality, race, sexuality, difference of all kinds, how and why we believe what we believe, that we might, beyond labels, find some common ground with our neighbor. Might we say hello and wish each other well as those solitary and communal paths cross from time to time."

Whether you're taking the slow lane or fast lane to arrive at your life's heartbeat, you'll probably find me, at some point or another, at a pit stop, welcoming you to a table to share a story, your story that makes you wholly unique and at the same time completely on common ground with the rest of us.

Elizabeth Blackshine, a Great Barrington resident, with a background as a mental health social worker, came to the written arts as a repeated column contributor to the Daily Guide of Accra Ghana, Rutgers Magazine, and On the Bridge, a collaboration between The Berkshire Eagle and Multicultural BRIDGE. Blackshine's reemerging passion is creative writing, working on her first play. Her professional background, travels, as well as steady resilience in recovery from chronic illness, inform her presence and creativity.

♥

Siobhan Connally - I felt that there were important stories that needed to be told and that it was an honor to be in a position to help tell those stories. There is an immense wisdom in such a collective. It has been an amazing experience to meet such diverse individuals, to listen to their stories and gain insight into what really enriches our lives as a community.

Siobhan Connally is a long-time writer and photographer living in Kinderhook, NY. Her work has appeared in The New York Times, Sports Illustrated, Arts and Antiques Magazine, Newsday, and The Artful Mind. Her weekly column about family life appears in The Record Newspaper in Troy. She is one of a team of freelance writers for On the Bridge, a collaboration between The Berkshire Eagle and Multicultural BRIDGE.

♥

JV Hampton-VanSant - In September 2001 at the mature age of 11 (and a half) and being of completely sound mind and sound body, I set a goal for myself: by the end of that year, I would write a book. After all, what else was a boy to do, especially one who was constantly using his imagination to build various worlds that only he could see, and stories only he could reenact. Whether it was creating my own set of wizard friends (a la "Harry Potter" or Diane Duane's "Young Wizard" series), or inventing my own superheroes, I reasoned that it would be selfish not to share these thoughts with anyone who would read them. Of course, as one would expect, most of these early creations have never (and will never) see the light of day. The artistic styling of an eccentric 11year old can only be so magnificent, and upon completion of my first set of stories, I realized that it would be better to practice before unleashing a masterpiece on the world.

Throughout the remainder of junior high school, high school, and college, I practiced writing in various forms: free-verse poetry, lyrics (with music), short stories, comic strips, scriptwriting, and even a small unpublished story series about a teenage vampire (in 2006, so long before it was cool and trendy). With time, and with the help of parents, mentors, and actual non-imaginary friends, I became less self-absorbed, and began to cherish stories that others made, stories that other people told. When I began to work for Multicultural BRIDGE, I came in contact with people from all different backgrounds, experiences, struggles and triumphs.

After posting every On The BRIDGE blog since its inception, I finally got my chance to conduct an interview. My first interview for On the BRIDGE was a collaborative one with Nik Davies on Jason Verchot. This was my first ever interview, and I was absolutely hooked. In addition to writing for BRIDGE, I am the BRIDGE Youth Diversity Leadership Coordinator/Trainer and the IT/Social Networking Coordinator.

On my own time, I am a Professional Merman Performer, educator and model, as well as a (human) model with Berkshire Beauty, LLC. I am also in the process of writing a series of children's books about life lessons learned by miniature merfolk living in a small aquarium, to be called One Tail at a Time. My main passion for working with young people is providing guidance for them toward a good path, inspiring them to be the best they can be at anything they do, reaffirming their potential and individuality, watching them succeed, and giving a little nudge forward here and there if needed. I am a lifelong Berkshire County native, and hopes to remain in the area for a very long time.

JV Hampton-VanSant has worked with BRIDGE in many capacities since 2008. Originally as a volunteer, he would help at events during summer breaks from college. As an intern, he managed the summer camp at Hevreh in 2011. Since graduating from Lesley University in 2012 with a BA in Holistic Psychology, he has worked as part of the administrative team as well as the primary youth leadership trainer. JV received his diversity training certification from the National Coalition Building Institute (NCBI) in the summer of 2012. Since then, he has received numerous other certifications, including sexual health and youth leadership. JV is also a professional merman performer, teacher, model, and soon-to-be children's book author working to encourage kids to actively engage with the world around them and make positive choices around diversity, environmentalism, and leadership.

♥

Roberta McCulloch-Dews - Good stories are hard to resist. So when I first learned of the opportunity to write for a new column series that aimed to tell the many stories of the Berkshires, I didn't hesitate to accept the offer. As a former newspaper reporter, I understood the power of a good story and its impact. On a personal level, I was relatively still new to the Berkshires, so this was also a great chance to learn more about the county. As a writer for On the Bridge, I had the privilege of traveling to different parts of county and heard fascinating stories and experiences from a cross-section of residents. It was clear the county possessed a diverse richness, and On the Bridge was a vehicle to sharing this treasure. After each interview, I always learned something new. It was apparent that while these stories obviously existed, they weren't necessarily part of the mainstream collective. Looking back, I am thankful to have been a part of this powerful series, and the role it's played in showcasing the Berkshires as home to many.

Roberta McCulloch-Dews is the owner of RMDews Media, a media consulting business. She has worked as a newspaper journalist for more than a decade throughout the northeast and has also worked in marketing communications at a global Fortune 500 company in upstate New York. Since moving to the Berkshires, Roberta has sought to participate in organizations that net a positive change in the community. In addition to the Berkshire County Commission on the Status of Women, Roberta is a member of the Women of Color Giving Circle of the Berkshires, the Lift E'vry Voice Advisory Committee, and she is a mentor through the Rights of Passage Program and the Multicultural BRIDGE Mentor Progam at Conte School. Additionally, Roberta is a 2013 graduate of the Leadership Institute for Political and Public Impact (LIPPI), offered through the Women's Fund of Massachusetts. Roberta received her B.A. in Print Journalism from New York University. She lives in Hinsdale with her husband, Warren, and three children, Warren III, West, and Kennedy.

Emma Sanger-Johnson - I first heard about the On the Bridge column when I began working with Multicultural BRIDGE in June 2014. As part of the project working on publishing the articles as a book, I quickly became very familiar with the stories of the people written about. As a relative newcomer to Berkshire County, I welcomed the chance to learn more. I was born in the suburbs of South Jersey, only a few miles from Philadelphia and moved to Great Barrington when I began studying at Simon's Rock. I decided to make this area my home for the near future. I wanted to learn more about this new community, so when asked to interview Pittsfield Police Chief Michael Wynn, I welcomed the chance to speak to a pillar of the Berkshire County community. BRIDGE reveals many facets of the community that may be unknown, ignored, unseen and unheard, and the column is integral to this work. My academic work focused on populations that were linguistically or culturally marginalized, focusing mostly on the Amazing in North Africa. The On the Bridge column is exciting to me because it is a project that ensures so many voices residing in Berkshire County are heard.

Emma Sanger-Johnson is recent graduate from Bard College at Simon's Rock. Emma has taught for BRIDGE in the past and joined as an Administrative Assistant Intern during the Summer of 2014. Currently, she works as a Special Projects and Outreach Coordinator for the organization working on the On the Bridge Anthology as well as writing a few articles.

♥

Jenn Smith -Both as The Berkshire Eagle's community engagement editor and as a Berkshire native, I see great value, purpose and thoughtful consideration in the "On the Bridge" partnership between Berkshires Week & Shires of Vermont and Multicultural BRIDGE. As a publication that strives to highlight the depth and breadth of culture, in every sense of the word, BWSV serves as an ideal vehicle for what Multicultural BRIDGE has worked for as an agency for change and understanding in our Berkshire backyard. Becoming a part of this collaboration just made sense. It has afforded me the opportunity to take the time to give a face to the individuals who fortify the backbone of this community.

Jenn Smith is the community engagement editor and education reporter for The Berkshire Eagle in Pittsfield, Mass. A 10-year veteran of the daily news outlet, Smith has covered a range of issues and events, from school, plays to standardized testing to the aftermaths of the 2012 Sandy Hook Elementary school massacre and 2013 Boston Marathon bombing. Smith has traveled from Pakistan to Haiti, returning with reports on humanitarian issues there. She is also a 2012 recipient of a Cultural Competency Award from Multicultural BRIDGE.

♥

Margot Welch - There is something about making a mark on a page. Writing was all I ever wanted to do. But, for as long as I've known this, I've also known I couldn't. At least not well enough. Even my diaries got very dull. I'd often start entries with, "This isn't really good writing but today…." I'd start poems with "If I were Whitman I might write about these lilacs…" or "Dear May Sarton. You left your clothes here last night, hanging to dry in my bathroom. They were too small for me or I might not write: so fiercely did I wish they'd fit."

Once, in fourth grade, I got permission to bring four friends into the Girls' Room at recess to tell them I'd started writing a play, called "All Men are Brothers." It was 1949. I didn't understand why my mother kept telling us this but decided it must be because not everybody knew - so we needed to be sure to tell people. In that antiseptic, tile-green bathroom I was excited and started explaining the script. Before I'd gotten very far, Joyce or Dawn or Patty began carping. "We don't want to learn anything by heart!" "I don't want to be an actress!" "I don't like pretending!" "How come you get to tell us what to do?" And finally, from one of them the lasting curse: "You're bossy!"

As they all turned to march out the door, like the Arab folding his tent, I stole away too. And shut up. I could keep writing. But speaking? Watch out what you say! I was a girl. In the 1950's. I would grow up. Good. And quiet.

My privileged life has given me precious opportunities for learning, serving, and purposeful writing. And, in my writing room, I have journals and journals, with folders and folders of unfinished poems and stories.

For the last two years, I've been answering the amazing invitation to stand with real writers, on a BRIDGE that - the same way Shelburne Falls' Bridge of Flowers celebrates the abundance of our earth - documents the beauty of multiculturalism in the Berkshires, linking all its diversities-on a real newspaper - to the welcoming community I love!

Writing—no matter what kind – has been my way to discover how things fit together, what I know, where I am. This BRIDGE, a place for me to stand, has led me to stories and friends, voices and histories I would never have known. Lives documenting courage, compassion, and the sustenance of traditions have showed me, over and over, how much we all share in our one small world. Indeed, all men and women are brothers and sisters: my mother was right. We are all connected. How much we have to write about - and care for. I am so grateful.

Margot Welch spent decades writing and working as a psychologist, counselor, and educator in court, community, school, and university settings. She's written op-eds and monographs about violence in schools, school-based services, and community schools, and a book, Promising Futures: the Unexpected Rewards of Engaged Philanthropy *(2006). Poems and fiction have appeared in Sojourner, Postcard Press, About Place and Persimmon Tree. She lives in Cambridge, Massachusetts.*

♥

Kuukua Dzigbordi Yomekpe I am a trans-disciplinary artist, choreographing West African dance forms, creating a fusion of Ghanaian dishes, and penning memoirs, essays, and social commentaries. I am the author of several essays and prose poems, some of which have been anthologized in: African Women Writing Resistance (UW Press), Becoming Bi: Bisexual Voices from Around the World (BRC), Pentimento, and Inside Your Ear (Oakland PublicLibrary Press). My Master's thesis, "The Audacity to Remain Single: Single Black Women in the Black Church," is anthologized in Queer Religion II (Praeger Publishers). My scholarly and writing interests lie at the intersection of race and skin color, African culture, Black women's bodies, expression of voice, and nonconformance and performativity. All my work is influenced by my education and socialization in womanist, feminist, and Africanist theories. I am a dancer and culinary artist, proud to be an African woman and a politically queer woman of color. I avidly feed a voracious travel bug that occupies the hinterlands of my soul, so I can often be found wandering various parts of the world.

Kuukua Dzigbordi Yomekpe has her hands in a few projects currently: The Coal Pot, *a Culinary Memoir celebrating her Ghanaian roots,* The Darker Sister, *a YA novel,* Musings of an African Woman, *her blog that features a collection of personal essays about Black women, social situations, immigration and assimilation, and a collaboration with On The Bridge and the Berkshire Eagle. She blogs at: ewurabasempe.wordpress.com and is a contributing blogger at: spoonwiz.com*

♥

Thank you to all of the contributors of the Berkshire Mosaic. You have shared your heart, lens, skill and time creating this living history project. ~ Gwendolyn

Epilogue

♥

A twig once taught a lesson about "community." The lesson: a twig, alone, cannot offer any resistance to the hands that gripped it at each end and then threatened to break it. However, when that twig is joined by other twigs of all sizes and of all shapes, there is now a "bundle" where there had been only one. Those that made-up the bundle, i.e., the community of twigs, they each were better protected, for each lent its strength to the whole. And so it is with Multicultural BRIDGE—One community joins hands with another; they in turn embrace a third and fourth and soon there is a mosaic made-up with children's smiles, adolescent's dreams, and adults' determined leadership. It has been said that to create something new, 1) the creation needs to be lovingly molded with the talent of the mind and hands; and, 2) the creation needs to be imbued with the enduring spirit of the brave. Those creations shaped by the talent of the mind and ready to withstand the test of time, were once the visions of visionaries. Such a creation conceived in love and imbued with the spirit of the brave, withstands the test of time because in the beginning it is undeniable that the visionary's vision was true. What else could then follow but the joining of a community? And so it has been with the Director of Multicultural BRIDGE.

Gwendolyn Hampton VanSant certainly must have had a vision of what could be and she asked, "Why not?" We see today what her good will and inner strength have given to the community. The participation of the residents of Berkshire County in the programs Gwendolyn has crafted goes back to 2009. During the years of 2009-2014, we have been enriched by her two Living History Projects, i.e., Living African American History Project; and the *Berkshire Mosaic: A Multicultural BRIDGE Living History Project*. Many participated in the "Dialogue about Race" as well as the "Multicultural BRIDGE Cultural Competence and Community Stewardship Awards Ceremony." The planning and directing of any one of these programs/projects would have been enough but not for Gwendolyn. This Berkshire community must surely bask in the light of knowing Gwendolyn and her staff are still present and on duty; the once separate communities nestled in the Berkshire Hills have walked down their pathways and joined hands and folkways together.

We live in a community with great diversity. For example, the collaboration between Gwendolyn and Kate Abbott of the Berkshire Eagle has resulted in an Eagle column "On the Bridge." The column's purpose is to introduce the readers to the diversity of people and passions in the Berkshires – from youth to the elderly, new residents to veterans, including Polish, Italian, Indian, Jewish, Irish, Latino, Native American and African Americans.

It must be that we all know that DIVERSITY derives its strength when each brings her/his folkway to a common table and all rejoice in their traits shared and the folkways so respectfully joined. This is the essence of Multicultural BRIDGE; this is its purpose; this is who we are.

Dr. Homer "Skip" Meade

W.E.B. DuBois Scholar
Larrywaug, Stockbridge

A Word from Kate Maguire

♥

On Sundays, you can find me or my husband Eric screaming at political talk shows or the New York Times newspaper. One particular Sunday, I read an article on the young men of ISIS where Thomas Friedman wrote, "They have never held a job or a girl's hand."

"That's for sure—held their hand?" I screamed. "They have utterly silenced their women, and they will ultimately not succeed because there is no woman's voice allowed, no mother or nurturer's voice," I screamed again. I screamed because I can. I screamed for them. You see, no women survive who scream at the men of ISIS. I guess I started screaming at a young age because when I was 4, my Greek mother trotted me off to drama lessons. Not to quiet me, but to contain and focus my vocal energy. Later, I learned my mother and her siblings could not speak English when they started school. Even back then, she understood that in order to succeed, one needed to speak and the more powerfully, the better. Mom was 88 when she passed in our home. In her final weeks I asked, "What was the proudest moment of your life?" She said, "It was when my parents became citizens of the United States. They were so happy, not for themselves, but because they knew we would all be safe. Make sure you keep screaming, Kathleen. Make sure you tell all those little kids in the theatre to keep screaming and remember where they came from." It was my mother's words that made me recognize I was part of some greater plan.

I love being an actress, producing great theatre, am thrilled when we can move a show to NYC, meet celebrities, but I also recognize a greater responsibility. In my role at Berkshire Theatre Group, I must open the doors of opportunity as wide as possible and we, collectively, must create a community that provides opportunities of growth for all our citizens. My mother, who I thought represented so many challenges in my life, had actually become a driving force. I now understand the legacy of the day that was the proudest of her life. Our forefathers and their generation have changed the world for us and the future will find its brightness as long as we keep clearing the path towards freedom.

Through the arts we understand what it means to be human and that the richness of our society lies in our diversity. This book wonderfully introduces us to our cultural inheritances. The ancients believed that the mystery of the human heart could be revealed by telling our stories. The gifts of such wise revelations may be found in the stories contained in these pages.

Kate

Board President of Downtown Pittsfield, Inc.
Artistic Director & CEO, of Berkshire Theatre Group

Appendix

"We are mosaics. Pieces of light, love, history, stars…Glued together with magic and music and words."

~Anita Krizzan

Learning Guide by Gwendolyn Hampton VanSant
Cultural Literacy & Storytelling Guide For All Readers

♥

In the words of Maya Angelou, "We can learn to see each other and ourselves in each other and recognize that human beings are more alike than we are unalike."

One can be asked to allow for another's beliefs, values, traditions and experiences without being asked to give up one's own beliefs, values, traditions, and experiences.

My goal in publishing this anthology is to let it serve as an educational tool for people of all ages increasing everyone's capacity to communicate across cultures. These *Berkshire Mosaic* stories do not tell a particular cultural group's full story but rather it gives us a snapshot of a moment in time, creating a living history of our diverse heritage in the United States. So often, cultural literacy seems like such a lofty goal, impossible to attain, and we worry about offending another if we don't know everything about a culture.

What Multicultural BRIDGE promotes is the capacity to understand another's experience, to walk in other shoes and for others to walk in ours. That is true tolerance in the sense of embracing cultural diversity. It is not putting up with another's existence but rather it is gaining the ability to really listen and understand another's experience. I, pursuing the role of cultural broker, first started in 2007 with the vision of shedding light on invisible communities and empowering voices of unheard individuals in our community.

Storytelling

As I wrapped up 2014's immersion in the study of positive psychology with Dr. Tal Ben Shahar and Dr. Maria Sirois, we landed on the importance of storytelling and in doing so I gained the language to explain why I was so compelled to find a home for our collective Berkshire stories. As we explored with Dr. Shahar, to understand and be understood and to know and be known are true keys to happiness and fulfillment; and as we journey through the *Berkshire Mosaic* experience, the joy of life and its offerings shine through. We travel alongside our storytellers and the words fill our imagination with sensations, smells, touch, and sights.

The premise of our anthology, supported by psychological research, is that stories are authentic human experiences and timeless links. Stories can connect us to ourselves and to a larger sense of belonging, history and existence. In positive psychology, we focus on the choice we have in every moment where one can frame one's story to evoke positive and happy emotions or sad and negative emotions. From time immemorial, stories have woven us together into a beautiful tapestry, or as someone recently said to me, layered us like the oils of a canvas masterpiece.

In The Psychological Power of Storytelling (Psychology Today 2011), Dr. Pamela B. Rutledge writes: Stories are about collaboration and connection. They transcend generations, they engage us through emotions, and they connect us to others. Through stories, we share passions, sadness, hardships, and joys. We share meaning and purpose. Stories are the common ground that allows people to communicate, overcoming our defenses and our differences. Stories allow us to understand ourselves better and to find our commonality with others.

Stories are how we think. They are how we make meaning of life. Call them schemas, scripts, cognitive maps, mental models, metaphors, or narratives. Stories are how we explain how things work, how we make decisions, how we justify our decisions, how we persuade others, how we understand our place in the world, create our identities, and define and teach social values.

Stories provide order. Humans seek certainty, and narrative structure is familiar, predictable, and comforting. Within the context of the story arc, we can withstand intense emotions because we know that resolution follows the conflict. We can experience with a safety net.

Stories are how we are wired. Stores take place in the imagination. To the human brain, imagined experiences are processed the same as real experiences. Stories create genuine emotions, presence (the sense of being somewhere), and behavioral responses.

Stories are the pathway to engaging our right brain and triggering our imagination. By engaging our imagination, we become participants in the narrative. We can step out of our own shoes, see differently, and increase our empathy for others. Through imagination, we tap into the creativity that is the foundation of innovation, self-discovery, and change.

Cultural Competence: The Platinum Rule

Treat others how they would like to be treated.

The Platinum Rule of Cultural Competence incorporates the Golden Rule as a starting point. But then it takes it one step further. Beyond treating someone how you would like to be treated (Golden Rule), one must use one's communication skills and positive intentions to find out how another would like to be treated. How do we do this? We present with a sense of interest and curiosity, absent of passing judgments. We give ourselves the gift of conversation and human connection like each of these interviews offers. There we develop cultural literacy. Beyond a label, we get to know people in our community that make up the mosaic.

Reflective questions

1. What does the interviewee want us to know about them?
2. How can you relate to the story you have just read?
3. What do I know about the culture, geography, history related to the story?
4. What did I learn from reading that profile or what will I research after reading it?
5. Reflect on the strengths and values of each interviewee. What were they able to do, what did they attain, what goals or dreams did they accomplish?

Children's Corner for Educators
Creating Mosaics

♥

Here are two options:

1. Decide on size and theme of a community art project in the form of a mosaic that you want to create. Ask each child to bring in a small item that represents a significant time in their lives. Have each child tell their story and then place their tile on the mosaic with glue or other adhesive. You can also have the child write a story depending on grade level and length of time.

2. Give each child a "tile" of construction paper in multiple colors. Have them design a tile about themselves and then explain to the class how that tile represents them. Then assemble all of the tiles into a mosaic.

These mosaics bring both a sense of community as well as developing literacy through storytelling and developing an appreciation for the diversity of each child.

Oral Storytelling and Cultural Literacy

♥

Through the storytelling in this book we have experienced how we can create greater understanding thereby creating community. Doriet Berkowitz shares in her NAYEC article, Oral Storytelling: Building Community through Dialogue, Engagement, and Problem Solving, the idea that, "Oral storytelling encourages a heightened and more sophisticated level of engagement...through its invitation for role-playing and performance...most are informally dramatized and brought to life through daily play and conversations among children. [Students] develop important speaking and listening skills when they express and respond to their own and others' ideas.

Experiences that arouse a deeper level of engagement and curiosity in a [student] and that propel the [student] to continue learning are valuable educational experiences (Dewey [1938] 1997). Oral storytelling and the dramatic play intertwined with it provide the foundation for children's educational experiences now and in the future. Educators can support [students'] cognitive, language, social, and emotional development by using...storytelling techniques."

Enjoy watching the young ones create community through sharing their stories via a mosaic with symbolic representation.

Multicultural BRIDGE has built several mosaics with children and youth in Berkshire County for you to view at:

Stearns Elementary School & BRIDGE summer program
Multicultural Bridges, a bilingual educational program.
Based on an image named, The Heart of Humanity

Lenox Public Schools and Lenox Middle School students
Based on the Pillars Of Character (Josephson's Institute) as part of
Multicultural BRIDGE's Pillars of Community initiative at Lenox Middle and High School

About Us

♥

We are Multicultural BRIDGE, Berkshire Resources for the Integration of Diverse Groups and Education, and we leverage community transformation by offering a comprehensive, unique and customized approach to facilitate bridging cultural norms and contexts.

Multicultural BRIDGE was co-founded in September 2007 by Marthe Bourdon and Gwendolyn Hampton VanSant with seed funds from Bob Norris, an incredible philanthropist in Southern Berkshire County of Western Massachusetts, who coined us 'catalysts for change,' Starting as an agency designed to bridge the gaps in service, we provide education and resources for both employees and employers. We transform culturally insensitive environments to culturally aware communities working towards cultural proficiency. As a State Vendor, we are also a Supplier Diversity Program or SDP. We hold certifications in education, cultural competence, multicultural awareness and interpretation/translation. We are a minority and women run non-profit organization and an Affirmative Market Program designed by the Governor of the state of Massachusetts. BRIDGE has been cited as a best practice model in community policing, education and family engagement. In 2015, BRIDGE has been cited as a best practice model for criminal justice in an undergraduate textbook and was revered as a model of applied research in the field of cultural competence amongst social psychologists in 2014.

BRIDGE promotes mutual understanding and acceptance among diverse groups and aims to serve as a resource to both local institutions and the community as a whole. BRIDGE strives to continue working as catalysts for systemic change and the integration of diverse groups through collaboration, education, training, dialogue, fellowship, and advocacy. BRIDGE's mission reflects transformation of workforce and community cultures to more integrated and culturally sensitive environments. Our model empowers diverse individuals to identify their own community resources, personal experience and assets needed to live a quality, safe, and integrated life.

[Governor] Patrick praised Gwendolyn's leadership, calling her and Multicultural BRIDGE "a treasure to Berkshire County and this Commonwealth. [BRIDGE] is doing a lot of important work welcoming immigrants and welcoming New Americans—which I think is so important—and dealing with issues around tolerance and working to build a stronger community," Berkshire Eagle July 7, 2010, Trevor Jones

Find us on the web

BRIDGE

BRIDGE413

Multicultural BRIDGE

Multicultural BRIDGE

Berkshire Resources for Integration of Diverse Groups and Education

Photo Gallery

♥

BRIDGE Woman to Woman Project participants with Director of WAM Theatre, Kristen van Ginhoven with BRIDGE Board Members, Dr. Eden-Reneé Hayes, Nik Davies and Gwendolyn at Barrington Stage, Pittsfield, MA

Dr. Brian Burke (Fairview Hospital), Wray Gunn, State Representative Smitty Pignatelli, BRIDGE Advisory Council Member at BRIDGE 5th Birthday Bash

Crystal Haynes, Greylock ABC Scholar and BRIDGE Diversity Leadership Participant at Mt. Greylock Regional High School, Williamstown, MA

Los Multicultural Dancers directed by Liliana Bermudez of Latino Festival of the Berkshires at the BRIDGE Award Ceremony at Shakespeare & Co.

BRIDGE Children's Educational Program, Multicultural Bridges at Housatonic School Site

BRIDGE Summer Children's Program at the Norman Rockwell Museum with guest Ty Allan Jackson

Youth Corps Member, Anissah Taylor with mom, Melanie and Ryan Blanchard, BRIDGE volunteer at the BRIDGE 5th Birthday Bash, Crissey Farms, Great Barrington, MA

Celebrating Ecuadorian Heritage in the Berkshires, a BRIDGE Multicultural Presentation

Migrations of the Heart - Berkshire Festival of Women Writers, with BRIDGE Women to Women Group

Rep. Pignatelli with MaryAnn Norris, BRIDGE Advisory Council Member and Bob Norris, Seed Donor & Co-Founder of Multicultural BRIDGE

Berkshire Chamber of Commerce, Reception for Governor Baker at Berkshire Museum, Pittsfield, Massachusetts

Dr. Eden-Reneé Hayes, BRIDGE Board Chair

Bob Norris and Antoine Alston, BRIDGE Volunteer, Small Business Supporter and Living African American History Project participant

BRIDGE Advisory Council: (left to right) Shirley Edgerton, Rodney Mashia, Rachel Branch, Ann LaBier, Natalie Shiras, Michael Wilcox, Marge Cohan, MaryAnn Norris

Natalie Shiras, BRIDGE Development Officer with Pauline Dongala, BRIDGE Volunteer of Global Academic Link (GAL) program

Gwendolyn with Advisory Council John Whalan and wife, Kate Gleason

BRIDGE Board Member Leandro Rosa and BRIDGE Volunteer Bonnie Oloff

BRIDGE Board: left to right Frances Jones Sneed, PhD, Lara Setti, MD, Lori Gazzillo, Gwendolyn VanSant, Mike Diaz, Dr. Eden-Reneé Hayes, and Estervina Davis

BRIDGE Program Students at Gateways Summer Learning Academy at Pittsfield Public Schools

Gwendolyn and Smitty at BRIDGE Cultural Competence and Community Stewardship Awards at Chesterwood in Stockbridge, MA

Gwendolyn with daughter, Jessica Hampton and BRIDGE Board Member Nik Davies with husband, Jimmy Hall at BRIDGE 5th Birthday Bash

Patricia Cambi with her daughter Yvonne, BRIDGE Youth Corps Intern and Gabriela Cruz with her husband, Armando Bautista

Race Task Force Members Joyce Armstrong and Natalie Shiras

Berkshire Mosaic Contributor Margot Welch with Gwendolyn

Annie Hampton and Nana Fran at BRIDGE Award Ceremony, Chesterwood

Kate Abbott, Berkshires Week Editor, with Gwendolyn and Rep. Pignatelli at Chesterwood

BRIDGE Mosaic by BRIDGE Summer Childrens Program Students

BRIDGE Childrens Educational Program with BRIDGE instructor, Veronica Johnston and Talya Taliaferro and Smergphy Olaverria at Norman Rockwell Museum, Stockbridge, MA

On the Climbing Statue at Norman Rockwell Museum

Dr. Frances Sneed, BRIDGE Board Member at Chesterwood

BRIDGE Youth Corps, Xinhui Li and Jennyfer Behanzin, teaching assistants at Summer Gateways Learning Academy

Celebrating Ecuadorian Heritage in the Berkshires, a BRIDGE Multicultural Presentation, Maria Soria and Patricia Cambi with her daughter

Morris Elementary School Student performing Peruvian Folkloric Dance at Renaissance Arts Center with BRIDGE Spanish Instructor, Veronica Johnston

Cecilia Allen, BRIDGE Spanish Interpreter and Instructor and family

Noah Elkin and wife, Barbara Krauthamer, BRIDGE Board President with Gwendolyn and Jessica Hampton

Marge Cohan with Rep. Pignatelli at Chesterwood

Dawn Durant Powell, Janis Broderick and Pamela Melendez of the Elizabeth Freeman Center at BRIDGE Awards Ceremony

Elder Nellie Gaulden and family at the Lift Ev'ry Voice Portrait of Elders Event at the Lichtenstein, Pittsfield, MA

Governor Patrick, Luci Leonard and Gwendolyn at BRIDGE's 1st annual Cultural Competence and Community Stewardship Awards Ceremony in 2010

Gwendolyn, Governor Deval Patrick and Eugenie Sills, BRIDGE Advisory Council Member

Gwendolyn with daughter, Jessica Hampton

Zach Robinette, BRIDGE Community Mentor at Conte School and Emily Vigiard, BRIDGE Community Engagement Coordinator at Lee Founders Day Race

Will Hampton at the BRIDGE 5th Birthday Bash

BRIDGE Strength in Community Forum Community Facilitators
at Pittsfield High School

Ariane Blanchard, Marge Cohan, Peggy Cooke, Lindsey Crawford, Otha Day, Mike Diaz, Sarah Gillooly, Iliana Hagenah, JV Hampton-VanSant, Bryan House, Nzima Hutchings, Barbara Mahony, Rodney Mashia, Ann O'Neil, Abdullah Abdul Rahim, Mulazzimuddin Rasool, Tes Reed, Natalie Shiras, Mark Siegars, Rachelle Smith, Tina Tartalagia with Gwendolyn, (not shown) Nik Davies, Ashley McNair, Taj Smith

♥

BRIDGE and its Race Task Force, under the leadership of Gwendolyn Hampton VanSant, confronted racial jeering of students, that occured at a school basketball game, with a focus on building community by facilitating in each classroom the first school-wide forums on Respect, Race and Strength in Community. The forum was led by BRIDGE-trained PHS faculty and community facilitators.

Kori Alston, BRIDGE Youth Corps at Norman Rockwell Museum.

Tymell and David of Railroad Street Youth Project

BRIDGE Real Talk at PHS with Youth Leaders, Andrew Otsuka and JV Hampton-VanSant

Tim Kiely of Pittsfield Co-Op Bank and BRIDGE Board President Lori Gazzillo

Larry Wallach, Morris Dancer with Ann Legêne and Sam VanSant

Stewart Burns, BRIDGE Advisory Council Member

Lila Berle and family at the BRIDGE 5th Birthday Bash

Olga Dunn Dancers at BRIDGE Award Ceremony, Shakespeare & Company

BRIDGE Board Treasurer, Mike Diaz with his children

Gwendolyn and the men of The Living African American History Project

Tom Alexander, Antoine Alston, City Councilor Churchill Cotton, Otha Day, Reverend Warren Dews, Jr., Wray Gunn, Chandrick Hayes, Rodney Mashia, Abdullah Abdul Rahim, Dr. Mulazzimuddin Rasool, Steve Robinson, Taj Smith, Dean Steve Sneed, Eddie Taylor, David Thompson and Chief Mike Wynn, (not shown) Ty Allan Jackson, Dr. Homer "Skip" Meade, Dr. Will Singleton

♥

The Living African American History Project began at Pittsfield High School on February 12, 2013, when nineteen distinguished African-American men from different professions discussed their careers and shared their life stories with hundreds of students.

The purpose of the project was to provide a community-based African American History Month experience as part of the BRIDGE Strength in Community Forum. BRIDGE and its Race Task Force, under the leadership of Gwendolyn Hampton VanSant, confronted racial jeering of students, that occured at a school basketball game, with a focus on building community by presenting the first school-wide forums on Respect, Race and Strength in Community. The forum was led by PHS faculty and BRIDGE-trained community facilitators. (see photo on page 157)

To fortify connections between PHS and the surrounding community, Gwendolyn took a proactive approach by designing the presentation of LAAHP which was comprised of some of the many African-American male role models in our community. Shown above are fifteen of the nineteen guest speakers that shared their voices and wisdom on that historic day.

Estervina Davis, Regina Rendon, Marta Escobar of BRIDGE Women to Women

Veronica Johnston, BRIDGE Instructor with BRIDGE Summer Program Students

Lift Ev'ry Voice 2013, Portraits of the Elders at the Lichtenstein Art Gallery, Pittsfield, MA

Professor Jonathan at Chesterwood

Don Quinn Kelley and Sandra Burton of Williams College

Sherry White

Natalie Shiras, BRIDGE Development Officer

State Rep. Pignatelli and Board President Lori Gazzillo

Mayor Jim Ruberto at BRIDGE Award Ceremony at Shakespeare & Company, Lenox, MA

Acknowledgements

♥

In deepest appreciation for all of the interviewees in this book who shared their story.

Thank you to Bob Norris and Marthe Bourdon in sharing in the vision and planting the seed for what is now Multicultural BRIDGE.

Love to my mother Annie Hampton and my father-in-law Nick VanSant.

Special thank you to Nik Davies who jumped in to make this book come together & flow and to Jimmy Hall for loaning me your wife and feeding me the best wings ever!

Special thank you to Kevin Moran and Kate Abbott for being our first ambassadors of this project to the public through the Berkshire Eagle collaboration with *On the BRIDGE*

♥

The Berkshire Eagle
Winnie Chen, The East Chinese Restaurant
Nik Davies & Eversource Energy
Zabian's Jewelers
Lenox Church on the Hill, United Church of Christ
Reverend Natalie Shiras
Nicholas P. VanSant
Natalie Hoerner
Ann Gallo
Grace Church
CiPP Kripalu
BRIDGE Staff, Board of Directors and
Race Task Force Members
First Annual BRIDGE Civil Rights Conference Sponsors
DeeAnn Veeder (proof reader extraordinaire, we love you!)

Special thanks to Bob and MaryAnn Norris and the Lennox Foundation for giving BRIDGE its foundation!

Current Employees

BRIDGE 2015

♥

Administrative Staff:

Gwendolyn Hampton VanSant, CEO and Founding Executive Director
Emily Vigiard, Outreach and Community Engagement Coordinator and Administrative Support
Estervina Davis, Family and Client Engagement Coordinator and Administrative Support
JV Hampton-VanSant, Youth Engagement Coordinator and Social Networking/IT Manager

♥

Instructors:
Stephanie Wright
Miguel Silva
Estervina Davis
JV Hampton-VanSant
Max Ehrman Shapiro
Karen Woolis

Interpreters:
Estervina Davis
Silvia Soria
Miguel Silva

Translators:
Xinhui Li
Peter Podol

Trainers/Facilitators:
Stephanie Wright
JV Hampton-VanSant

Accounts Manager:
Erin Coty

Development Officer:
Natalie Shiras

GAL Coordinator:
Pauline Dongala

Alphabetical Index

A

Abbas, Asma	43
Adams, Maggie	101
Adawulai, Mohammad	103
Alston, Kori	45
Ananda, Satyana	3

B

Belalcazar, Alexandra	63
Bethel- Smith, Nakeida	105
Bonvillain, Nancy	47
Breindel, Rabbi Josh	25
Brown, Eiko	73
Burns, Stewart	49
Burton, Sandra	5

C

Cami, George & Irinia	27
Chen, Winnie	75
Conklin, Will	33
Cruz, Gabriela	29

D

Dupont, Austen	33
Durant, Reverend Willard	101
Dzigbordi- Yomekpe, Kuukua	69

E

Enchill, Alfred	77
Estime, Kiana	95

F

Fernandez, Luis	63
French Jr., Harold P.	7
Fulop, John	79

G

Gillooly, Sarah	109
Golden, Minnie & Cornelius Jr.	31
Greene, Hilary	9
Grossman, Jo	13
Guerrero, Grace & Luis	83

H

Hartman, Saidiya	111
Haynes, Crystal	33
Heath, David	51
Hellman, Paula	35
Herrick, Samantha	53
Hicks, Brian D.	11

J

Jonathan, Darius	57

Alphabetical Index (cont.)

K

Kelley, Don Quinn	5

L

LaBier, Ann	13
Larson, Karran	113

M

Maguire, Sue	15
Mahida, Jignesh	81
Makuc, Mary	60
McHugh, Bear	61
Meade, Homer "Skip"	87

Q

Quizhpi, Lucia	29

R

Robinson, Steve & Bill	37
Rotondo, Ralph & Jeannette	115

S

Sblendorio, Christopher	17
Sirker, Yvette "Jamuna"	39

S (cont.)

Sekowski, Maria & Kris	89
Sholes-Ross, Reverend Sheila	117
Shaw, Reverend Edward	65
Slaughter, Nyanna	67
Sonsini, Joe & Theresa	91
Soria, Maria	29
Syldor-Severino, Will Amado	119

U

VanSant, Nicholas	17
Verchot, Jason	121

W

White, Sherry	19
Wilcox, Chief Richard	19
Wright, Stephanie	31
Wynn, Chief Michael	93

Z

Zabian, Mike & Mary	97
Zimmerman, Reverend Janet	21